ArtN

YELLOW
PAGES

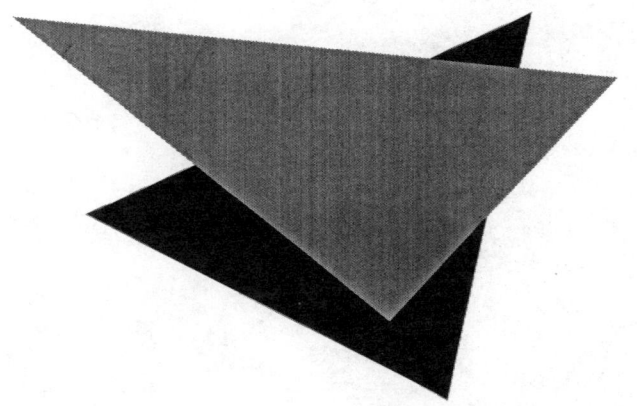

ArtNetwork

YELLOW PAGES

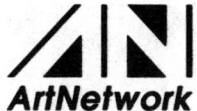

ArtNetwork

Published by ArtNetwork
PO Box 1268, 18757 Wildflower Dr
Penn Valley, CA 95946
916/432-7630 916/432-7633 Fax

*ArtNetwork is a publishing company whose
aim is to connect fine artists with artworld
professionals. In addition to publishing art
marketing books and newsletters, ArtNetwork
sponsors seminars across the country.*

*All entries for this edition were selected by the
editor, not solicited. To be listed in future
editions, send appropriate materials to the
address noted above.*

Cover Design by Richard Moore

DISCLAIMER *While the publisher and editor
have made every reasonable attempt to obtain
accurate information and verify same, with such
a large volume of references occasional address
and telephone number changes are inevitable
as well as other discrepancies. We assume no
liability for errors or omissions in editorial listings. Should you discover any changes, please
write the publisher so that corrections may be
made in future editions.*

Publisher's Cataloging in Publication
(Prepared by Quality Books Inc.)

ArtNetwork yellow pages/ [edited by]
Constance Smith.
  p. cm.
  Includes index.
  ISBN 0-940899-25-6

1. Artists–Services for–Directories. 2. Arts–
Equipment and supplies–Directories. I. Smith,
Constance, 1949- ed. II. ArtNetwork

N8351.A77 1995   700
                         QB195-20284

Table of Contents

How to Use This Book

We are pleased to present to all fine artists and artworld professionals the concept of a Yellow Pages for the Artworld. You will keep and reference this book for years to come.

Though you may think you will not need to "read" this directory from cover to cover, we suggest you do! Be sure to have a highlighter in hand, and mark those items of interest to you. You will find many clues to your marketing needs within areas you might not have suspected. So read the entire book!

Send away for the multitude of free catalogs listed and start a reference file for your own use. (Be sure to tell them ArtNetwork sent you!)

The guiding idea behind this resource book is to make it easy for you to find the help that you need; whether it be art supplies, slide labels, restoration, framers, networking organizations, employment or any of a myriad of other resources.

This directory brings together, from thousands of sources, a compilation that is organized and simple to use. We've left margins so you can write notes (and do write in the book!). An entire month was spent on the phone verifying telephone numbers just before going to press, so they are the most current they could possibly be at press time. Though we do list 800 numbers when we have them, we have noticed that many companies disconnect their 800 number after only a brief use (probably due to costs!) If you find a listing where this is the case, call their local number or write them for more information.

We know we have left out some important resources—of course not intentionally! If you know of sources we have left out, be sure to send us information so we can add them to the next edition!

Constance Smith, Editor

CHAPTER 1

RESOURCES

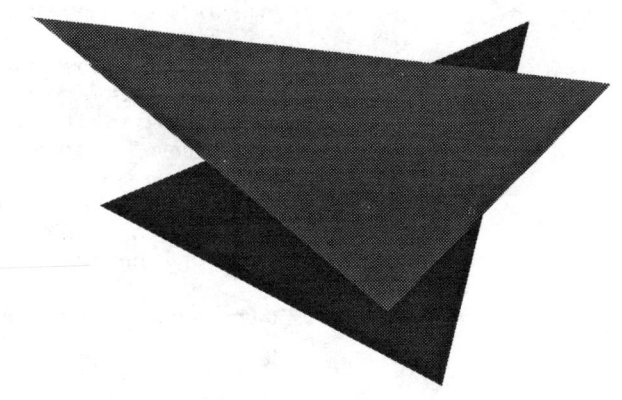

Appraisers

American Society of Appraisers/ASA
AW Carson
Box 17265, Washington, DC 20041
703/478-2228
Multidisciplinary, members include appraisers of fine arts. Publishes a newsletter and an accredited directory of appraisers.

Appraisers Association of America
386 Park Ave #2000, New York, NY 10016
212/889-5404

Art Appraisal, Restoration & Consultation/AARC
EJ Epstein
33 Park Dr, Mt Kisco, NY 10549
914/666-7690

Art Consultant Associates
Lila Held
13800 Shaker Blvd #804, Shaker Heights, OH 44120
216/561-4420

Bernard Ewell
318 E Cache La Poudre, Colorado Springs, CO 80903

Carmichael and Carmichael Fine Art
Gil Carmichael
308 Prince St, St Paul, MN 55101-1437
612/225-8970

Carten & Associates
Marilyn Carten
4107 Rosedale Ave, Austin, TX 78756
512/452-0210

International Society of Fine Art Appraisers
Elizabeth Carr
3339 N Overhill Ave, Chicago, IL 60634-3122
815/848-3340

National Institute of Appraisers/NIA
Box 69301, Los Angeles, CA 90069
800/676-2148 310/289-1148

Paul Sternberg
2120 Cornerstone Ln, Marietta, GA 30064
404/426-7647

Telepraisal
Box 20686, New York, NY 10009
800/645-6002 212/614-9090

Archival Products

20th Century Plastics
800/767-0777
Office and photo organizers.

Archivart
800/804-8428
Call for catalog of archival products.

Century Archival Products
804/644-7824
Beautiful boxes you can use to make your portfolio.

Conservation Materials
PO Box 2884, Sparks, NV 89431
702/331-0582

Conservation Resources
8000H Forbes Pl, Springfield, VA 22151
703/321-7730

Gaylord Brothers
PO Box 4901, Syracuse, NY 13221
800/448-6160 315/457-5070

Graphic Dimensions Ltd
41-34 Haight St, Flushing, NY 11355
800/221-0262
Archival framing supplies.

Hollinger Corp
PO Box 8360, Fredericksburg, VA 22404
703/898-7300

Judson Art Warehouse
Masterpak
49-20 Fifth St, Long Island City, NY 11101
800/922-5522 718/937-5500

Light Impressions
800/828-9859

Stock Solutions
307 W 200 St #3004, Salt Lake City, UT 84101
801/363-9700

TALAS
568 Broadway, New York, NY 10012
212/219-0770
Conservation supplies, marble paper, and free materials.

University Products
517 Main St, Holyoke, MA 01041-0101
413/532-3372

Resources

Auctions

This is only a partial list of auctions throughout the year. Many times local organizations or media networks will sponsor local auctions. These can be a good way to put your artwork in the eyes of local patrons. Donating a work does not necessarily mean you receive no money for it. Be sure you ask for 30-50% of the bid. ArtNetwork has a more complete mailing list of auction houses available for rent at $25. Ask for a brochure by calling 916/432-7630.

Arabian Horse Trust
Mary Lou Walbergh
5838 Bonsall Dr, Malibu, CA 90265
213/457-7323
Original Western art.

Art Promotion Ltd
1040 Bayview Dr #430, Ft Lauderdale, FL 33304

Butterfield & Butterfield
220 San Bruno Ave, San Francisco, CA 94103

Christie's East
219 E 67th St, New York, NY 10021

Citadel Gallery
PO Box 720098, San Jose, CA 95172-0098

CM Russell Auction
Deanne André
PO Box 634, Great Falls, MT 59403
406/761-6453

European Auction House
68670 1st St, Cathedral City, CA 92234

Harness Track of America
Chris McErlean
35 Airport Rd, Morristown, NJ 07960
201/285-9090
The only art exhibition and auction devoted solely to the Standardbred Rising Stars.

Jeffrey Burchard & Associates
2528 30th Ave N, St Petersburg, FL 33713
813/821-1167

New England Fine Art Auctions
Malcolm Seymour
Evergreen Ln, Box 15, Hopedale, MA 01747

Rocky Mountain MS Charity Art Auction
National Multiple Sclerosis Society
PO Box 556, Casper, WY 82602
307/234-2340

Santa Monica Auctions
2044 Broadway, Santa Monica, CA 90404
310/453-9196

Silkirk's
4166 Olive, St Louis, MO 63108
314/533-1700

Skinner Inc
357 Main St, Boston, MA
508/779-6241

Sotheby's Inc
1334 York Ave, New York, NY 10021

Swann Galleries
104 E 25th St, New York, NY 10010

Washington Project for the Arts/WPA
400 7th St NW, Washington, DC 20004
202/347-4813
Send slides to Auction Selection Committee around March. Auction is in November.

Wolf's Auction Gallery
1234 W 6th St, Cleveland, OH 44113-1301

Computer & Software Services

AproposART
George Hoffman
167 Elm Ave, Woodlynne, NJ 08107
Stores and links information on artworks.

ArtAccess
11000 Metro Parkway #33, Ft Myers, FL 33912
813/939-2425

ArtFact
1130 Ten Rod Rd #E104, N Kingstown, RI 02852
401/295-2656
100 auction houses/1 million auction records; Subscription service via CD ROM.

Artistsavenue
1730 Blake #300, Denver, CO 80202
303/292-2230

Artists-on-Line
6311 N O'Connor #N53 Bldg III, Irving, TX 75039
800/605-6333

ArtQuest
314/567-5226

Art Gallery PC System
Flamingo Software
5359 E Weaver Dr #101, Littleton, CO 80121
303/220-8052

The Art Manager
12443 Beech Fork Ln, Athens, AL 35611
205/729-6909
Computer software application for artists/$39.95.

Art Systems Ltd
17 W 17th St #603, New York, NY 10011
212/741-1906

Art Trak
2916 McKinney Ave, Dallas, TX 75204
214/979-0009
On-line systems for galleries, museums; soon for artists.

Canned Art Connection
210 Cutler St, Allegan, MI 49801
Computer clip art resources.

Centrox Corp
145 E 57th St, New York, NY 10022
800/278-6397   212/319-4800

Clip Art Connection, ConnectSoft
6741 185th Ave NE, Redmond, WA 98052
800/234-9497

Collage Collections
951 Old County Rd #196, Belmont, CA 94002
415/594-1285
Electronic art portfolios.

Comphoto
703/765-4562
Floppy disk portfolios.

Encompass Fine Art Systems
5424 N 74th St, Scottsdale, AZ 85250

Encore International
18 E 16th St, New York, NY 10003-3111
212/741-1906

Faben Inc
1290 Palm Ave, Sarasota, FL 34236
Organizes business on PC for artists; awards, sales, inventory, etc.

Infovision Technologies
18 Lyman St #I, Westborough, MA 01581
508/366-3660
Imaging and info cataloguing software/interfaces directly into software/$125.

PC Views
PO Box 2164, Fair Oaks, CA 95628
800/PC-VIEWS 916/961-9773
Produces a high-quality reproduction of a photo or artwork to use as your screen saver. $24.95 for first photo; each additional image is $5.95. You'll need a color monitor.

Scanning New York
Art Today Video Magazine
6 Erita Ln, Smithtown, NY 11787-1305
800/578-2466

SecureTrack
800/277-9600
Conveniently catalogues information with integrated video, scan or file images of your most valued collectibles.

Technology Management Resources/TMR
212/243-3553

VisionWorks
800/617-9955 713/465-7626

Resources

Employment in the Arts

Also see page 72 for books in this area.

Access
30 Irving Pl 9Fl, New York, NY 10003
212/475-1001
Maintains a database of job openings in non-profit organizations.

American Association of Museums/AAM
AVISO
1225 Eye St NW #200, Washington, DC 20005
202/289-1818
The best source for administrative openings in museums. $33/year, $3/single issue.

Artist Resource Letter
School of the Museum of Fine Arts
Career Services
230 The Fenway, Boston, MA 02115
617/369-3635
A newsletter that has jobs, grants, residency resources and other information/$20.00/6 months.

Artjob
WESTAF
236 Montezuma Ave, Santa Fe, NM 87501
505/982-0532 505/988-1166
Subscription newsletter. $30/6 months.

Artlinks
Marti Klinkner
PO Box 223, Berkeley, CA 94701
510/528-2668
Employment agency for the arts.

Artsearch
355 Lexington Ave, New York, NY 10017
212/697-5230
National Employment Service Bulletin for the Arts; $54/year (2x a month).

College Art Association/CAA
275 7th Ave, New York, NY 10004
212/691-1051
Referral service for listings of positions available in the college system in art-related fields. Must be a member in order to get the publication.

Community Arts News
Alliance of Ohio Community Arts Agencies
77 S High St 2Fl, Columbus, OH 43215
614/241-5327
Free.

Current Jobs in the Arts
PO Box 40550, Washington, DC 20016
703/506-4400
$19/3 monthly issues.

DC Art/Works
410 8th St NW, Washington, DC 20004
202/727-3412
The only arts employment program in the nation. Training programs in the arts.

Delaware Division of the Arts
820 N French St 1Fl, Wilmington, DE 19801
302/577-3540
Has a listing of current employment in the arts. Available to view during office hours.

National Art Education Association/NAEA
1916 Association Dr, Reston, VA 22091-1590
703/860-8000
Publishes "Teaching Art as a Career," a $2.00 brochure.

National Guild of Community Schools of the Arts/NGCSA
PO Box 8018, Englewood, NJ 07631
201/871-3337
Referral service in visual arts education. Job descriptions sent to members. $60/membership.

North Carolina Arts Council
Dept of Cultural Resources, Raleigh, NC 27601
919/733-2111
Monthly listings of jobs around the country/3 months free.

Opportunity Resources Inc
25 W 43 St #1017, New York, NY 10036
212/575-1688
National Executive Search and Placement Agency. Has listings of positions available in the college system for art-related fields. Must be a member in order to get this publication.

Seattle Arts Commission
221 First Ave W, Seattle, WA 98119
206/684-7171

Short Subjects
Greater Philadelphia Cultural Alliance
320 Walnut St, Philadelphia, PA 19106
215/440-8100
Most listings for greater Philadelphia area. $20/year.

Framers & Suppliers

Look for local frame shops in the yellow pages. Many advertise in your local arts newsletters or art magazine too.

Arquati
3308 Garden Brook Dr, Dallas, TX 75234
214/243-0201

Art Systems
Salvatore Cutrono
113 E Union St, Pasadena, CA 91103
213/681-2401
Packaging crates.

The Cutting Edge
Total At Home Picture Framing Press
PO Box 826, Island Lake, IL 60042
708/526-0030
A four-page newsletter of tips and techniques. $24.95/ year. Holds workshops on matting techniques throughout the country. If you want to save money and have great-looking frames, do-it-yourself!

Easy Leaf
947 N Cole Ave, Los Angeles, CA 90038
213/469-0856
Gold leafing and frame products.

FrameWealth
RD 2 Box 261, Otego, NY 13825
800/524-8582

Frame Factory
800/621-6570

Frame Styles
2107 Penn Ave S, Minneapolis, MN 55405
612/374-2420

Franken Frames
609 W Walnut, Johnson City, TN 37604
800/322-5899 615/268-8653

Imperial Picture Frames
PO Box 598, Imperial Beach, CA 91933
800/423-2620

Kenneth Lynch & Sons
84 Danbury Rd, Wilton, CT 06897
203/762-8363
Manufactures a special hanging rod system for museums, homes and galleries.

Larson Juhl
3900 Steve Reynolds Blvd, Norcross, GA 30093
404/279-5200
Large distributor of frames. Call for their free catalogue.

Making and Decorating Fantastic Frames by Thom Boswell
Sterling Publishing Co
387 Park Ave S, New York, NY 10016
$14.95.

Master Framers
262 E 4th St, St Paul, MN
612/291-8820

Metropolitan Picture Framing
6959 Washington Ave S, Edina, MN 55439
800/626-3139

Museum Classics
Donald Fonger
5051 W Jefferson Blvd, Los Angeles, CA 90016
213/731-7536

New Haven Lighting
PO Box 6353, Hamden, CT 06517
800/243-3123
New concepts in lighting art.

Royal Picture Frame
Mike Desai
4122 Weston Rd, Weston, Toronto, Ontario
Canada M9L 1W7
416/742-7425
They do specialty moldings, including carved frames to fit any environment.

S&W Framing Supplies Inc
120 Broadway, Garden City Park, NY 10040
800/645-3399
Ask for catalog of gallery rods.

TraCom International
Wayne Hung
307 Serendipity Dr #B, PO Box 1223,
Millersville, MD 21108
410/987-2198
Sells special hanging systems for frames.

Walker Display
250 S Lake Ave, Duluth, MN 55802-2304
218/722-5945
Display rods.

Resources

Hazards in the Arts & Recycling

These organizations have literature to inform you of possible hazards and recycling info. See page 71 for reference books on the topic.

Access Re-Use It!
Resource Center
2517 W Pine St, PO Box 4652, Tampa, FL 33677
813/875-6754

Art & Craft Materials Institute/ACMI
100 Boylston St #1050, Boston, MA 02116
617/426-6400
Provides information to artists and public.

Artists Foundation
860 Harrison Ave #309, Boston, MA 03127
617/859-3810

Cedar-al Products
800/431-3444
Tired of styrofoam peanuts? Light-weight cedar chips for packing, recycling and burning when through.

Center for Safety in the Arts
5 Beekman St #820, New York, NY 10038
212/227-6220
Has brochures and pamphlets for sale on various topics. Works with waste management and disposal in schools.

Conservatree
10 Lombard St #250, San Francisco, CA 94111
415/433-1000
Carries recycled papers, bulk only; could be good for unusual portfolio covers.

East Bay Depot for Creative Reuse
1027 60th St, Oakland, CA 94608
510/547-6470

Eastco Industrial Safety Corp
800/929-1000
Industrial safety supplies. Call for brochure.

Environmental Defense Fund
800/225-5333
Leave your name and address, and they will send you a packet of recycling info.

Global Safety
516/625-4466

Imagination Market
528 Powell St, Vancouver, BC Canada Y6A 1G9
604/983-9686
An 11,000-square-foot front with workshop, warehouse and gallery space. Five van loads of materials are collected each week.

Lab Safety Supply Co
800/356-0722

Natural Kraft Collection
Gift Box Corporation of America
225 Fifth Ave, New York, NY 10010
800/GIFT-BOX
Recycled boxes and bags.

Ranpak Corp
20220 87th Ave S Bldg I, Kent, WA 98031
206/872-6890
Designer-oriented, environmentally safe packaging materials.

Recycle
Boston Children's Museum
300 Congress St, Boston, MA 02210
617/426-6500

Recycle Market
Los Angeles Children's Museum/Helen Marish
310 N Main St, Los Angeles, CA 90012
213/687-8801

Trash Art
Materials for the Arts/Susan Glass
2 Columbus Cir, New York, NY 10019
212/841-4100
A joint project of the NY City Dept of Sanitation and Dept of Cultural Affairs which links material donations to non-profit organizations and individual artists in need of paint, paper, office equipment and industrial by-products.

Hotlines

Visual Artists Information Hotline
American Council for the Arts
800/232-2789
Mon-Fri 2-5 EST. A referral service which can tell you who to contact regarding funding, housing, insurance, health, law and general resources.

Law Hotline
900/555-ARTS
This 900 number has about 75 art law topics: copyright; artist; gallery relations; commissions; logos; protecting an artist's style; taxes; insurance; moral rights; print disclosure laws, etc. $1.95 per minute.

New York Gallery Highlights
212/777-ARTS
Can advertise for $65 per month.

Housing

Arthouse
Ft Mason Center C-255, San Francisco, CA 94123
415/885-1194
A clearinghouse for information about artists' studio and live/work space. Call for information about publications and ongoing workshops.

Artplace
212/226-3760
A studio space with 16' ceilings available in Long Island. A new project is starting in Manhattan.

CAA Newsletter
Reneé
275 7th Ave, New York, NY 10001
212/691-1051 ext. 251
A publication that lists rentals and exchanges in Europe.

Maria Walsh Sharpe Art Foundation
711 N Tejon St #B, Colorado Springs, CO 80903
719/635-3220
Subsidizes studios in New York City.

Loans

Artists Community Federal Credit Union
155 Ave of the Americas 14Fl, New York, NY 10013
212/366-5669
A bank for artists and the artworld! Many other benefits.

Artists Fellowship Inc
Arthur Harrow, President
47 Fifth Ave, New York, NY 10003
212/255-7740
For disabled artists. Call between 12-1 EST.

Artists Foundation in Boston
860 Harrison Ave #309, Boston, MA 03127
617/859-3810
Manages the Artist Emergency Loan Fund which provides both no-interest and low-interest loans of up to $500 for artists who need help.

Merchant Status

Receiving credit card status as a small merchant can sometimes be difficult. If you do outdoor shows, it is especially helpful for sales to accept credit cards. Establish a business account at your bank. Approach them with a merchant status request. If they won't give it to you, go to your local credit union. Often they have more flexibility in this area.

American Express
800/528-5200

Cardservice
800/944-7164
A company that you can pass your VISA/MC/AmEx through (for a charge). If it's the only way to be able to accept credit cards, it might be worth it!

Carte Blanche/Diner's Club
800/525-7376

Discover Card
800/347-6673

First National Bankcard Services
5880 E State St #135-188, Rockford, IL 61108
815/969-7255

National Association of Credit Card Merchants
407/737-7500
To receive merchant status for VISA/MC.

Practical Solutions Ltd
Box 5221, Gainesville, Fl 32602
904/372-1569

US Wireless Data
4888 Pearl E Cir #110, Boulder, CO 80301
800/979-3282   303/440-5464
Lease, rent or purchase options available for check and charge verification.

Resources

Insurance Companies

As you become established in your career, insuring your work and business becomes more and more important. Following are some companies and organizations to contact if you're at that point. Some art organizations provide group-type eligibility for coverage, both health and liability.

If you have a problem or complaint, contact your state's insurance commission as well as:

• **All Risk Brokerage**
111 John St, New York, NY 10007
212/385-4300

• **Insurance Information Institute**
110 William St, New York, NY 10038
800/221-4954

• **National Insurance Consumer Organization**
344 Commerce St, Alexandria, VA 22314
703/549-8050

Allen Insurance Associates
5750 Wilshire Blvd #525, Los Angeles, CA 90036
800/488-9040 213/933-3770

American Craft Council/ACC
PO Box 3000, Danville, NJ 07834
800/562-1973

American Federation of Arts
41 E 65th St, New York, NY 10021
800/AFA-0270
'Artsure' offers discounts on fine art insurance.

Associated & Society Insurance Corp
Susan Barnes
11400 Rockville Pike #500, Rockville, MD 20852
800/638-2610

Associated Underwriters
PO Box 20086, St Petersburg, FL 33742
800/328-2317
General liability insurance for outdoor art shows.

CA Associated Insurance Brokers
Laura Marley
55 Hawthorne #500, San Francisco, CA 94105
415/543-0890
Competitive rates.

Fine Arts Risk Management Inc
225 W 34th St #1715, New York, NY 10122
800/795-8075

Flather and Perkins
Bruce Perkins
888 17th St NW, Washington, DC 20006
800/422-8889

Frenklel & Co Inc
123 William St, New York, NY 10038
212/267-2200

Henderson Phillips Fine Arts
800/871-9991
Mostly for museums and galleries.

Hogg Robinson of New York Inc
355 Lexington Ave, New York, NY 10017
212/682-7500

Huntington T Block Insurance
1120 20th St NW, Washington, DC 20036
202/223-0673

Marsh & McLennan
1166 Ave of the Americas, New York, NY 10036
212/345-5000

Mutual of Omaha
Mutual of Omaha Plz, Omaha, NE 68172
800/624-5554

National Artists Equity Association/NAEA
PO Box 28068, Central Station, Washington, DC 20038
800/727-6232
Write or call for their membership and non-membership insurance policies.

Reliance National
77 Water St, New York, NY 10005
212/338-2524

Trinder & Norwood
106 Corporate Park Dr, White Plains, NY 10604-3301
914/694-5600

Wolfgram/Tritt & Associates
1633 Oakdale Ave, Box 18218, W St Paul, MN 55118
612/451-9565

Miscellaneous Products

ABC Pictures
1867 E Florida St, Springfield, MO 65803
Quantity reprints of B&W or color photos.

Action J Marketing
26 Firemens Memorial Dr #201A, Pomona,
NY 10970
Luggage tags made from your business card. Five tags at $3 each/$15.

Artkart
1105 Bellevue Rd, Atwater, CA 95301
209/358-9011
"Kartboard" protects the face of your painting.

AWI Adonis
1020 Calle Cordillera #102, San Clemente,
CA 92673
They make a paint-brush carrying bag that keeps you organized. $29.95.

Black Forest
8604 E Houghton Lake Rd, Merritt, MI 49867
616/328-4478
Oil paint and brushes at great prices.

Business Book
800/558-0220
Photo labels/50 for $12.95.

Checks in the Mail
PO Box 7802, Irwindale, CA 91706
800/733-4443
Great looking styles—much better than your local bank—and much cheaper/$6.98 for 250 checks.

CKS
1115 N La Brea Ave, Inglewood, CA 90302
310/677-3775
Stretcher bars.

Color Q
PO Box 1007, Dayton, OH 45401
800/999-1007
Customized calendars of your artwork.

Concepts Limited
22 Church St #103, Ramsey, NJ 07446
Luggage tags made from your business cards.

Deluxe Business Forms
PO Box 35100, Colorado Springs, CO 80935
800/328-0304
Personalized Post-it notes. $12.95 for 10 pads.

Deluxe Life Style Management Products
800/533-3383
MemoryBank Personal Organizer.

Dick Allyson
21 Cote Dr, Epping, NH 03042
603/679-5266
Title plaques for as little as $40—great for adding that final touch to a painting.

Direct Promotions
23935 Ventura Blvd, Calabasas, CA 91302
818/591-9010
Plastic coated rolodex cards.

Documentation Holders
212/860-0091

Dovetail Design
1509B Leslie Ave, Alexandria, VA 22301
703/739-2804
Fine art display easels.

Drawing Board
800/527-9530
Office supplies.

Exposures
1 Memory Ln, PO Box 3615, Oshkosh, WI
54903-3615
800/222-4947
Picture storage.

Fidelity
800/328-3034
Office supplies.

Fileworks
Charlie Kessler
95 Vandam St, New York, NY 10013
212/989-5687
Great bargains on recycled light tables, typewriters and office furnishings.

Fine Arts Stretcher Bars
500 Molino St #214, Los Angeles, CA 90013
213/625-8031

FLAX
PO Box 7216, San Francisco, CA 94120
800/547-7778
Silver and gold metallic pens that adhere to leather, vinyl or dark paper. They also have a personal embosser which could make your business letterhead look great at $20. Call for free catalog.

Resources

Miscellaneous Products (cont.)

Foto Fabric Impressions
10 Bonnie Dr, Northport, NY 11768
800/745-8735
Printing on caps, T-shirts, sweat shirts, mugs, etc.

Freund Can Co
190 W 84th St, Chicago, IL 60620
312/224-4230
Mailing tubes in quantity.

Gibson Displays
122 White Dogwood Ln, Statesville, NC 28677
704/873-8121
Print bins.

Gill Mechanical Company
PO Box 7247, Eugene, OR 97401
503/686-1606
Tube Wringer—ends the waste of half-used tubes.

Grayarc
PO Box 2944, Hartford, CT 06104-2944
800/243-5250
Office supplies.

Guy DeVaney
7226 W Colonial Dr #111, Orlando, FL 32818
407/297-9517
16-month calendars, 4x3' wall size.

Hold Everything
800/421-2264
Ask for free catalog of items for organizing your office.

Home Office
800/869-6000
Catalog of modern office supplies.

Hop Inc
2330 Southfield Rd #3, Mississauga, Ontario
Canada
905/821-7550
Various sizes of plastic envelopes to protect prints.

Image Innovations
7685 Washington Ave S, Minneapolis, MN 55439
800/345-4118
Photo supplies, storage goods, software for slide labels. Ask for free brochure.

Impact Images
4961 Windplay Dr, El Dorado Hills, CA 95762
800/233-2630
Crystal clear bags for storing, could be used for packaging greeting cards, etc.

Industrial Paper Tube
Harold Kramer
1335 E Bay Ave, Bronx, NY 10474
718/893-5000
Mailing tubes.

Island Graphics
PO Box 16502, Seattle, WA 98116
206/563-4661
Computer mouse pads custom-made from your artwork or photo.

Jam Paper Corp
111 3rd Ave, New York, NY 10003
212/473-6666
Designer-color tyvek envelopes. $75/1000, a bit more than usual but could be effective for an attention-getter!

JasBag
800/657-8166
Carrying case for watercolor paintings.

Jerry's Art-a-Rama
248-12 Union Turnpike, Bellerose, NY 11426
800/U-ARTIST 718/343-0777
T-shirts from your photos, up to 11x17".

Jim Bell
1322 Walla Walla, Wenatchee, WA 98801
Custom color photographic prints, 11x14"/$4.40.

John Bannon Inc
PO Box 104, Fairfax Station, VA 22039
"Maroger Medium" for oil painting.

Kim Fiori
24100 Beverly Dr, Quail Valley, CA 92587
909/244-7624
Line portraits and drawings for advertising, etc.

Label Store
800/257-8354

Mailers
Jack Christensen
40650 Forest View Rd, Zion, IL 60099
800/872-6670 708/872-6677
White cardboard mailers.

McSmith
612/342-4488
Packaging and display products.

Metro Associates
PO Box 7685, Rutherford, NJ 07073
800/343-4423
Display bins.

Metrotype
200 Gate Five Rd #102, Sausalito, CA 94965
415/331-2956
Personalized calendars, note cards and book-marks, as well as T-shirts—the whole gamut.

Midwest Photo Co
402/734-7200
Prints at affordable prices: 25 B&W 5x7" @ .92

Miles Kimball
41 W 8th Ave, Oshkosh, WI 54906
"Midas Touch" marking pens that write in gold and silver/$2.89.

Monroe Specialty
PO Box 740, Monroe, WI 53566-0740
Engraved name plates for paintings.

MWM Dexter Inc
Rose Stevens
800/641-3398
Rolodex/postcard—great for promotion purposes at $325 for 1000.

National Bag
800/247-6000
Packaging supplies.

Nelson Marketing
PO Box 320, Oshkosh, WI 54902-0320
800/722-5203
Note pads, etc. with engraved names/reasonable prices.

Paragona
PO Box 3324, Santa Monica, CA 90408
800/991-5899
Glass palettes.

Pictureframe Products Inc
34 Hamilton Rd, Arlington, MA 02174
800/221-0530
Manufactures a mini-wrap shrink packager.

Plastic Bags Mart
511 Excelsior Ave E, Hopkins, MN 55343
800/727-7618
Plastic bags for outdoor show merchandise.

Presentation Systems
951 Hensley, Richmond, CA 94801
510/236-8882
Display bins.

Quill
800/789-1331
Office supplies.

Reliable Home Office
800/869-6000
Press-On Mini Pix—turn your favorite artwork photo into a picture sticker for your envelopes, business cards, flyers and brochures.

Rice Paper Box Company
Gene Rice
530 Acoma St, Denver, CO 80204
303/825-8287
Notecard boxes with clear lids.

Rosencrantz & Guildenstern Banknotes
PO Box 150, Milford, NH 03055
800/354-4708
Exceptional designed checks; i.e. Van Gogh, Monet, Munch, Michelangelo, amongst others. 200 checks/$18.

Rubber Stamp & Seal Inc
PO Box 2258, Wichita, KS 67201
316/682-5511
Various stamps, including one with the Copyright © mark.

SCS Company
PO Box 2024, Huntington, WV 25720-2024
800/942-9304
Special extender for oil paints.

Selwyn Textile Co Inc
134 W 29th St, New York, NY 10001
Linen and cotton canvases.

Sign Design
280 Regency Ct #201, Brookfield, WI 53045
800/274-9161
Quality engraved nameplates for paintings.

Resources

Miscellaneous Products
(cont.)

Signs by Paul
11082 S Milliken Ave, Conifer, CO 80433
303/697-8003
Name plates for your finished, framed paintings.

Sisyphus Art Supply
800/872-2545
Stretcher bars.

Smith Art Inc
PO Box 700, Palm Harbor, FL 34682-0700
813/787-4700
"Smartbox," a custom-crafted artists' sketchbook.

Southgate USA
359 Wales Ave, Bronx, NY 10454
800/347-2008
Display bins.

Stephen Foster Co Inc
439 S Dartmoor, Crystal Lake, IL 60014
800/762-0017
Unusual embossed seals, reasonably priced.

Successful Advertising
10016 Biddulph Rd, Cleveland, OH 44144
216/456-8606
Banners.

Sy's Work Clothes
6689 Orchard Lake Rd #284, W Bloomfield,
MI 48322
810/738-9519
*Artists' smocks —$7-9—slightly used and worn,
but look like new.*

Tampa Tube Containers Inc
800/785-TUBE
Mailing tubes.

Taylor Importing Co
Tim Taylor
24 Fourth St, Valley Stream, NY 11581
Linen fabrics.

Testrite Instrument Co Inc
135 Monroe St, Newark, NJ 07105
Easels, light boxes, exhibition lights, projectors.

Twin Brook Professional Stretchers
RR 1 Box 5444, Lincolnville, ME 04849
800/856-1567 207/763-4271

United States Postal Service
Philatelic Fulfillment Service Center
PO Box 419208, Kansas City, MO 64141
*Offers logo-imprinted envelopes with postage in
small quantities at a reasonable price.*

University Productions
517 Main St, PO Box 101, Holyoke, MA 01041
800/628-1912
Photo supplies.

USA Inc
333 Kimberly Dr, Carol Stream, IL 60188
*They will duplicate a photo or slide onto a label
which you can put on an envelope, invitation,
etc. Write for information.*

Utility
PO Box 217, 144 Main St, Gardiner, NY 12525
914/255-9290
Canvas.

Verilux
PO Box 2937, Stamford, CT 06906
800/786-6850
True-balanced full-spectrum studio lighting.

Vilmann and Decker
PO Box 807, Palm Springs, CA 92263
800/247-2544
*StretchMaster™ is a reusable aluminum frame
that comes in stock silex.*

Watercolor Backpack
800/348-2338
$112 + s&h.

William Soghor Co
PO Box 6366, New York, NY 10128
Index cards for documenting your artwork.

World Market Inc
2011 E Fifth St #4, Tempe, AZ 85281
*"Photobackers," labels that are printed on and stick to
the back of a photograph to make it into a postcard.*

Xpander Pak
275 N Field Dr, Lake Forest, IL 60045
*Nylon and polyurethane packing envelopes that
inflate, protecting fragile items; reusable.*

Yazoo Mills Inc
PO Box 369, New Oxford, PA 17350
800/242-5216 717/624-8993
Mailing tubes.

Packers & Movers

Gallery Association of New York State
Box 345, Hamilton, New York, NY 13346
315/824-2510
They put out a small brochure entitled "Art on the Move" ($10ppd) which lists fine art shippers, packers and warehouses across the U.S. and what they do. Your local house mover probably can also recommend a fine art shipper in your area. Don't trust the regular movers. They don't know what 'fine art' is and how to pack it. Look in your local art magazine or Yellow Pages for people advertising this service.

A-1 Babber Packing and Crating
8231 W 3rd St, Los Angeles, CA 90048
213/651-3241

Airfloat Systems
Mitzi Pergman
110 Elizabeth St, PO Box 229, Tupelo, MS 38802
800/445-2580
Foam- and plastic-lined, corrugated shipping containers for framed fine art or prints.

Allied Van Lines
Special Products Division
300 Park Plaza, Naperville, IL 60563
708/898-1100

ArtCrate
213/681-2401
Very sturdy shipping crates.

Art Handlers
Sharon Pattison
1570 Pacheco St #E14, Santa Fe, NM 87501
505/982-0228
Expert transportation, storage and installation.

Art Move Ltd
Unit 3 Grant Rd, London, SW11 2NU
England

Art Moves Incorporated
225 NW 26th St, Miami, FL 33127

Art Source International
1237 Pearl St, Boulder, CO 80302
303/444-4080

Artech Inc
Bob Bean
2609 First Ave, Seattle, WA 98121
206/728-8822

Artex Inc
7117 Maple Ave, Takoma Park, MD 20912

Artlines
PO Box 4825, West Hills, CA 91308
818/884-4886
Museum-quality art handling.

Atlantic
1001 Wilson Dr, Baltimore, MD 21223

Atthowe Fine Arts Services
926 32nd St, Oakland, CA 94608

Troy Thompsen Associates
650 8th St, Hermosa Beach, CA 90254
310/372-2445
Specializes in installation and security. Also manages rotation of collections.

Authentic Frame & Arts Services
251 Heath St, Boston, MA 02130

Complete Art Services
1711 N Lakeside Dr, Lake Worth, FL 33460
407/624-4060

Contemporary Installations
449 N Oak St, Inglewood, CA 90302
310/673-7200

Cooke's Crating Inc
3124 E 11th St, Los Angeles, CA 90023
213/268-5101

Curatorial Assistance
213/681-2401
Cost-effective art crates and protection for shipping of art.

DAD Trucking
S I Guinard
76 Varick St, New York, NY 10013
212/226-0107
Dealing exclusively in art. Full-service facility in New York City; storage, packing, inventory consolidation and transportation.

Fine Arts Express Inc
251 Heath St, Boston, MA 02130
617/566-1155

Fine Arts Express SW
465 W 38th St, Houston, TX 77018

Resources

Packers & Movers (cont.)

Fine Arts Express SW
7440 Whitehall, Ft Worth, TX 76118
817/589-0855 803/571-1444

Grosso Art Packers
1400 York Ave, New York, NY 10021
212/734-8879

Hahn Bros
212/926-1505
Fireproof warehouses.

Hardy Built System
PO Box 351, Ambler, PA 19002-0351
Manufactures very sturdy boxes for shipping fine art.

Hudson Shipping Co
17 Batter Pl #1230, New York, NY 10006
212/487-2600
Fine art packing, customs clearance, export forwarding, air and sea. Licensed custom-house brokers and international freight forwarders.

ICON Group Inc
417 N Sangamon, Chicago, IL 60622

International Cargo Systems Inc
Fine Art Division/Laura Rogers
PO Box 457, E Boston, MA 02128
617/561-1171

Judson Art Warehouse
Tom Pelham
49-20 Fifth St, Long Island City, NY 11101
800/922-5522 718/937-5500
High security, climate-controlled storage and trucking, packing/crating, travelling cases, import/export, freight forwarding and installation. Send for free brochure of archival materials for packing and shipping.

LA Packing & Crating
Jim Isenson
5722 W Jefferson Blvd, Los Angeles, CA 90230
213/937-2669
Fine art packing, crating, warehouse storage, receiving, delivery, shipping and packing supplies.

Len Art
6620 Leland Wy, Hollywood, CA 90028

Marshall Fine Arts West
Larry Hulse
1062 Revere Ave, San Francisco, CA 94124
415/467-3628

Mayflower Fine Arts Division
4836 SE Powell Blvd, Portland, OR 97286

More Specialized Art Transportation/Morart
222 Bargen Tnpk, Ridgefield Park, NJ 07660
201/641-2500

Museum Services
2921 Como Ave SE, Minneapolis, MN 55413
612/378-1189

Ollendorff Fine Arts
780 E 138th St, Bronx, NY 10454
718/937-8200

Parma Movers Inc
3584 W 67th St, Cleveland, OH 44102

Racine Berkow Associates
375 W Broadway, New York, NY 10013
212/226-2411
Fine art shipping, specializing in international transport of art and museum exhibitions. Licensed US custom broker.

Regency Worldwide Packing
John Taylor
33-31 Greenpoint Ave, Long Island City, NY 11101
718/729-8877
Exclusively engaged in managing fine art transportation, crating and shipping worldwide or across town.

Security Storage
Conrad Reid
1701 Florida Ave NW, Washington, DC 20009
202/797-5615
Moving and storage in temperature control vault.

Transport Consultants International
37 Elm St #8, Westfield, NJ 07090
800/752-7002 908/789-8923
Complete fine art shipping service, domestic and international.

West Coast Keating
William Lappas
9665 Wilshire Blvd #700, Beverly, Hills, CA 90212

Portfolio Materials

Portfoliobox Inc
166 Valley St, Bldg 3-402, Providence, RI 02909
401/272-9490
Specialize in custom folios and boxes.

Treaty Oak Press
851 Dairy Ashford, Houston, TX 77079
800/327-2162 713/497-4661
Foil-printed presentation folders.

Promotional Materials

Carrot Top Industries
437 Dimmocks Mill Rd, PO Box 820, Hillsborough, NC 27278
919/732-6200
Flags, banners, etc.

Fixturecraft
443 E Westfield Ave, Roselle Park, NJ 07204
908/245-8440
All-purpose counter displays.

NEBS Inc
500 Main St, Groton, MA 01471
508/448-6111
Stock bags for outdoor shows, etc.

Unity Screen Printing
406/257-5056
Banners, etc.

Publicity Firms

Amelia Associates
William Amelia
8 W Madison St, Baltimore, MD 21201
410/727-3100

Art Media Intl
1365 York Ave #28E, New York, NY 10021
212/794-1200

Bellas Artes International
Barbara Wichmann
341 Benton St, Santa Rosa, CA 95401
707/473-3702

DLM Intermedia
310/572-6561
Public relations and promotions for people in the arts. Offices in New York and Canada as well as Los Angeles.

Fabri Creations
Karen Perry
110 Mast Rd, Falmouth, ME 04105
207/797-4288
Conducts workshops on press kits and getting publicity.

Howard J Rubenstein Associates
1345 Ave of the Americas, New York, NY 10105
212/489-6900

Irene Aimee Depke
5627 N Neva Ave, Chicago, IL 60631
312/774-2589

Marcia Yudkin
PO Box 1310, Boston, MA 02117
617/438-5918
Publishes information on getting publicity.

New Directions
Millie Szerman
409 N Pacific Coast Hwy #900, Redondo Beach, CA 90277
310/798-8990

Public Relations to the Arts
Laura Segal
212/966-1997
Ten years experience in press and media campaigns for visual arts. Also writes grants, fundraising and career development.

Rogers & Cowan
2233 Wisconsin Ave NW #500, Washington, DC 20007
202/338-1900

TransMedia Consultants
Thomas J Madden
6001 Broken Sound Pkwy NW #414, Boca Raton, FL 33487
407/998-4888

Resources

Restorers & Conservators

American Institute for Conservation of Historic & Artistic Works
1717 K St NW #301, Washington, DC
202/452-9545

Art Conservators
Guy Downing
13500 Takara Rd, Chico, CA 95928
916/343-2787
Restoring and gold-leafing.

Avery Gallery
Shae Avery
390 Roswell, Marietta, GA 30060
404/427-2459

Bronson Fine Arts
1410 2nd St, Santa Monica, CA 90401
310/587-2577

Eva Matysek Fine Art Restoration
4016 W 242nd St, Torrance, CA 90505
310/540-4429
Restoration and conservation of oil paintings.

Fine Art Care and Treatment Standards/FACTS
415/472-0800   415/472-2841

Fine Art Conservation Inc
Jerry Jiritano
192 Toronto Ave, Massapequa, NY 11758
516/798-6336

Nathan Zakheim & Associates
PO Box 408, Culver City, CA 90232-0408
310/280-0596
Scientific art conservation.

National Institute for the Conservation of Cultural Property
3299 K St NW #602, Washington, DC 20007
202/625-1495

Pennsylvania Art Conservatory
Philip Rosenfield
636 Lancaster Ave, Berwyn, PA 19312
610/644-4300
Restoration of paintings and prints, including wax-resin linings, full cleaning and repairs. Prints cleaned, repaired and deacidified. Member of International Association of Conservators.

Theft Information Services

Art Guard
5777 W Century Blvd #110, Los Angeles, CA 90045
310/337-7779
Anti-forgery devices.

Art Loss Register
13 Grosvenor Pl, London SW1X 7HH
071/235-3393
Has a data bank of 35,000 lost or stolen works in its files. For $20, dealers, individual buyers or museums can register a stolen work.

Art Theft Update
A periodic column in the Wall Street Journal.

Foundation for Art Research
46 E 70th St, New York, NY 10021
212/879-1780
They publish Stolen Art Alert, a newsletter that keeps people posted on stolen goods. $50/1 year. They also offer an art theft search service and an art authentication service.

PSI Tech
Ryan Wood
806 Port Walk Pl, Redwood City, CA 94065
A psychic team that helps locate missing art pieces. $100,000 reward minimum.

Spiel Associates
Robert Spiel
155 N Michigan Ave #500, Chicago, IL 60601
312/861-1313
Publishes a newsletter "Art Intelligence." Had a 20-year career with the FBI in the recovery of stolen fine art and rare collectibles.

Slide Duplication

Citizens Photo
PO Box 15068, Portland, OR 97215
503/232-8501
10 dupes for $4.10. (Includes critical color match.)

Fuji TruColor
PO Box 52008, Phoenix, AZ 85072
1-9 dupes for .29, 10-24 @.25. (Shipping and handling add $3.00.)

Midwest Photo Co
Tanya Weyers
4900 G St, Omaha, NE 69117
800/228-7208

NY Dupes
167 Avenue B #1-F, New York, NY 10009
212/473-4600
10 dupes for $10.75.

PhotoGenesis
Ray Young
3425 Balboa St, San Francisco, CA 94121
415/386-3735
Prints from slides, 5x7" @$9.

Replichrome
89 5th Ave #903, New York, NY 10003
212/929-0409
First slide $1.75; each additional $1.00.

The Slide Factory
Ed Silver
300 Broadway #14, San Francisco, CA 94133
415/957-1369
11 dupes for $7.60.

Slide Labels

Artists' Labels
Al Agnew
1117 Leisure Ln #2, Walnut Creek, CA 94595
510/944-6362

Creative Edge
Diana Clarke
PO Box 662, Alpine, NJ 07620
201/784-7977
Also produces brochures, etc.

Hannah Does It!
Hannah Chauvet
510/528-6386

RMG Labels
Rosalyn Gaier
6598 Glenallen Ave, Cleveland, OH 44139
216/248-8341
Send SASE for brochure and sample of labels.

Slide Labels
212/969-0147

Slides/Photographs

Image International
Paul J Moshay
16935 Vanowen St #C, Van Nuys, CA 91406
818/881-1774

Ronnie Haber
301/656-8787

Studio on the Go
310/441-1923

Slide Storage

Barkes Products
5245 W Clinton Ave, Milwaukee, WI 53223
800/223-1357 414/354-9000

Elden Enterprises
PO Box 3201, Charleston, WV 25332-3201
800/950-7775

Multiplex
1555 Larkin Williams Rd, Fenton, MD 63026
800/325-3350

Resources

Tapes & Videos

Alternative Marketing Options & Developing Art on Screen
Program for Art on Film/Columbia U
2875 Broadway 2Fl, New York, NY 10025
212/854-9570
Catalogs all videos related to art.

Art Video Library
PO Box 68, Ukiah, OR 97880
503/427-3024

Artists InterActive Video Productions
2400 Rio Grand #1-210, Albuquerque, NM 87104
Drawing videos.

Artists' Video Productions
97 Windward Ln, Bristol, RI 02809
800/648-1602

Arts America
9 Benedict Pl, Greenwich, CT 06830
800/553-5278   203/869-4694
Over 300 videos of contemporary and old masters.

Bravo
150 Crossways Park W, Woodbury, NY 11797
516/364-2222
A news program, "ArtsBreak," that travels to local communities.

Chesney Communications
Bob Chesney
2302 Martin St #125, Irvine, CA 92715
714/756-1905
If you want to produce a video tape, this person can help you!

Collage and Assemblage
800/200-RT4U

Craven Home Videos
Michael Craven
PO Box 4012, Hollywood, CA 90078
818/562-1739
This set of 12 videos was made for college classroom use, to assist artists to learn how the real art market works; includes interviews with artworld professionals.

Crystal Productions
Box 22159, Glenview, IL 60025
800/255-8629
Educational videos in the arts.

DeHavilland Fine Art
ArtNetwork
916/432-7630
Two video tapes produced by a gallery owner on the East Coast: "Five Steps to Get Your Art in a Gallery" and "Three Steps to Sell Your Art on Your Own."

Dove Enterprises
4520 Hudson Dr, Stow, OH 44224
800/233-3683

Facets Video
1517 W Fullerton, Chicago, IL 60614
800/331-6197
Rare art videos.

Printing and Cassette Services
6211 S 380 W, Salt Lake City, UT 84107
801/265-9393
Duplicates audio and video tapes; prints books and labels.

Scanning New York Art
Art Today Video Magazine
6 Erita Ln, Smithtown, NY 11787-1305
800/578-2466
Ten times a year a fresh cassette to keep you on top of the art scene; includes up to 30 current and upcoming exhibitions and as many as 180 full-color images.

Signilar Art Videos
PO Box 278, Sanbornton, NH 03269-0278
800/205-4904   603/934-3222
Educational videos.

Six Steps to Success
ArtNetwork
916/432-7630
60-minute audio tape by Sue Viders and Steven Doherty with practical advice for marketing; sells for $19.95.

Tapette Corporation
5 Whatney, Irvine, CA 92718
714/588-7000
Complete duplication services for audio and video tapes.

Time Wave
  800/762-0343 619/238-5234
  Color awakening series.

V-Corporation
  1228 E Edna Pl, Covina, CA 91724
  800/V-CORP-99 818/966-0412
  Audio and video duplication.

Video for the Arts
  Angela Fernan
  274 Court St, Brooklyn, NY 11231

Video Learning Library
  15838 N 62nd St #101, Scottsdale, AZ
  85254-9888
  Business videos.

Video Learning Library
  5777 Azalea Dr, Grants Pass, OR 97526
  503/479-7140

Video Preview
  Scanning NY Art/Art Today Video Magazine
  6 Erita Ln, Smithtown, NY 11787-1305
  800/578-2466
  30 top NY galleries.

VIS
  1111 Secaucus Rd, Secaucus, NJ 07094
  800/223-0433 201/867-7600
  Video duplication fulfillment.

Telephones

American Telephone Tapes
  1695 Florida Mango Rd, W Palm Beach, FL
  33406
  800/358-2543 407/439-4177
  Voicemail with 8 boxes. 1-line $249/2-line $289.

Voice Mail
  800/675-9005
  Private boxes are $5.95 per month with a $15 installation fee. Available in most areas of the country.

GBH Distributing
  701 W Harvard Wy, Glendale, CA 91204
  800/222-5424 818/246-9900
  Headsets without cords! Only $298.

800 Numbers
  800/555-1212
  Directory assistance for companies that have 800 numbers

Directories
  800/544-4988
  Need a directory from another city that you'll be visiting? Order and have them billed to your phone bill.

Directory assistance
  1/area code/555-1212
  65¢ per call for 2-3 inquiries.

Call Trace
  Dial *57, and the number of the last call you received will automatically be reported to the telephone co. Useful if you have harassing calls. $1 per use.

Caller ID Block
  Dial *67 (1167 from rotary) before you talk; your name and telephone # will not be displayed on the caller ID-equipped phone. No charge.

Repeat Call
  Dial *66, and your phone will automatically re-dial a busy number for up to 30 minutes. When you hear a special ring you will recognize your call going through. 50¢ per use.

Return Call
  Dial *69, and your phone will automatically dial the number of the last phone number which was used to called you (local calls only). Good for when you can't get to the phone in time to answer it. 75¢ per use.

CHAPTER II

BUSINESSES
LAWYERS
&
ACCOUNTANTS

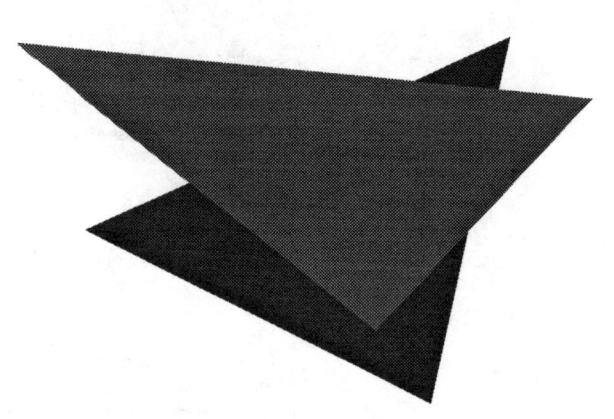

Many of the following organizations assist artists with general business, accounting, tax and legal problems. Some of the organizations hold seminars on various business matters as well as being an information center, often having a library available to the public. Some of the people/ organizations listed give artists a discounted fee (or perhaps a trade!).

For more information on legal rights as an artist, read pages 55-60 and 155-162 of Art Marketing Handbook for the Fine Artist (published by ArtNetwork).

Seminars

Several training organizations offer simple bookkeeping, management and organizational seminars around the country. Call for their free brochures.

Skillpath 800/873-7545
CareerTrack 800/334-1018
National Seminars Group 800/258-7246
Fred Pryor Seminars 800/255-6139

Start-up Kits

Many Chambers of Commerce are set up to assist citizens with developing their business. Contact your local Chamber to see how they can help you. The city of Chico, CA, for instance, has a start-up kit for $30ppd that contains all the forms needed to set up a sole proprietorship.

Chico Chamber of Commerce
PO Box 3038, Chico, CA 95927
916/891-5556

Copyright Office

Library of Congress, Washington DC 20559
202/707-9100 (forms) Ask for form 'VA'
202/479-0700 (assistance)

IRS

800/829-1040
Call for free tax guides for small businesses.

Office of Consumer Affairs

Securities & Exchange Commission
450 Fifth St NW #2115, Washington, DC 20549
202/272-7440
If you have a complaint or problem with brokers, financial advisors, money managers, etc., complain here.

Sales and Use Tax Department/Board of Equalization
Look in your local directory under your state government listings. This is where you apply for and file your sales tax return.

Business Volunteers for the Arts/USA

Arts and Business Council
25 W 45 St, New York, NY 10036
212/819-9287
They have 31 affiliate branches around the country.

Small Business Administration/SBA

Mail Code 7110
409 Third St SW, Washington, DC 20416
800/827-5722 (800/8ASK-SBA)
Look in your local yellow pages for the office nearest you. Call for brochures on business topics. Some areas have a program called SCORE, in which retired executives help you in their area of expertise.

SBA Management Administration

PO Box 15434, Ft Worth, TX 76119
817/885-6500
Free booklets to assist in business tactics; call for free catalog.

Better Business Bureau/BBB

202/393-8000
Look in your local directory for the office nearest you.

Credit Reporting Agency

Dun & Bradstreet
800/234-3867

National Artists Equity Association/NAEA

PO Box 28068, Central Station, Washington, DC 20038
800/727-NAEA

Accountants for the Public Interest

1012 14th St #906 NW, Washington, DC 20005
202/347-1668
Small Business Development Centers exist all over the country. Income tax assistance is also available in many cities for low-income individuals. They also have a National Directory of Volunteer Accounting Programs.

American Institute of Certified Public Accountants

1211 Ave of the Americas, New York, NY 10036
212/575-6200
If you have a problem or complaint against any accountant, complain here, as well as to your state's accountant board.

Businesses, Lawyers & Accountants

ArtLaw Line
VLA
1 E 53rd St 6Fl, New York, NY 10022
212/319-2910
Publications, seminars, internships for law students interested in going into arts and entertainment law. Artist Legacy Project for artists with HIV/AIDS to assist them in estate planning.

ARTlaw Hotline 900/555-ARTS
Kaufman & Silverberg
918 16th St NW #400, Washington, DC 20006
202/466-2787
The 900 number has about 75 art law topics: copyright; artist/gallery relations; commissions; logos; protecting an artist's style; taxes; insurance; moral rights; print disclosure laws, etc. $1.95 for the first minute.

ArtNetwork
916/432-7630
Mailing list on pressure sensitive labels of 100 businesses and lawyers for the arts/$25.

National Business Incubator Association
20 E Circle Dr #190, Athens, OH 45701
614/593-4331
This is the headquarters of what is called "the incubator system" which assists and directs small businesses to locations in their area that will assist them with their small business needs.

User-Friendly Agreements

The first time I ever wrote an agreement as an agent for an artist's commission, I copied verbatim a contract from a legal guidebook for artists. Within hours after giving it to the potential client, I realized the drastic error. She read it thoroughly and had several hesitations. I didn't even know what some of the things I had included meant! After I spoke to her and calmed her down, she finally signed the agreement. I was lucky! I had almost lost a commission.

Since then I have abided by 'user-friendly' agreements—basically a letter that states, in simple layman terms, the rights of the artist. When completing a sale, I suggest that artists include this information on their invoice or sales receipt. It's important for artists to keep track of who they sell a work to and where it in turn might be sold or given as a gift or trade. When your retrospective exhibition comes up in twenty years, you'll want to know where that piece of artwork is! Your clients will respect the idea that you want to keep track of your work (i.e. that you intend to become known).

It is good to understand at the onset of any business relationship what is expected of all parties concerned.

When a gallery wants an agreement, what do you do? Write a formal (but user-friendly!) letter of agreement. Send it by registered return-receipt mail. If they disagree with part of it, they will respond with their suggested terms.

What to Include in a Sales Agreement Letter

• How to take care of a particular type of artwork (i.e. out of the sun, under glass, not hung over the fireplace, non-destruction and modification clause, etc.)
• Your reproduction rights
• Resale information (i.e. name and address of any new owner)
• Right to go to the location of artwork to photograph
• Right to re-acquire work for brief periods for retrospective exhibition purposes
• Royalty on re-transfer of artwork
• A share of rental income or a limitation on exhibition of the artwork.

Businesses, Lawyers & Accountants

Publications on Legal Matters

*Names and addresses of publishers of books noted with an asterisk following their name are listed in the section "Art Business Book Publishers." Titles with ** previous to name denote books that ArtNetwork sells (916/432-7630).*

An Artist's Guide to Small Claims Court
NY Lawyers for the Arts

An Artist's Handbook on Copyright
Georgia Volunteer Lawyers for the Arts
42 Spring St SW, Plz Level 16, Atlanta, GA 30302

Art Law and Accounting Reporter
Texas Accountants for the Arts
1540 Sul Ross, Houston, TX 77006
713/526-4876
A newsletter.

The Art Law Primer by Linda Pinkerton and John Guardalabene
Lyons & Burford*

Art Law: Representing Artists, Dealers and Collectors by RE Duffy

The Artist's Friendly Legal Guide by Floyd Conner, Peter Karlen, Jean Perwin and David Spatt
Northlight*

Artists Legal Source Book by Toby Klayman

ArtsFirst
Susan Stephan, Editor
4233 Crocker Ave, Edina, MN 55416
612/927-7492
Newsletter.

Beauty and the Beast: On Museums, Art, the Law and the Market by Stephen E Weil

**Business and Legal Forms for Fine Artists by Tad Crawford

Contracts for Artists by WR Ginnilliat

Copyright Basics by US Copyright Office
Copyright Information Kit
Library of Congress, Washington, DC 20559
202/479-0700

The Copyright Book: A Practical Guide by William S Strong

Copyright Handbook by DF Johnston

Law and the Arts by Horwitz

**Legal Guide for the Visual Artist by Tad Crawford

LEGALease
Center for Nonprofit Management
U of St Thomas
52 Tenth St S, Minneapolis, MN 55403-2001
612/962-4300
A quarterly newsletter for nonprofit managers and boards.

Licensing Art & Design by Caryn R Leland

Make It Legal by Lee Wilson

**Making It Legal by Martha Blue

Protecting Your Heirs and Creative Works: An Estate Planning Guide for Artists, Authors, Composers and Other Creators of Artistic Works by Tad Crawford

Taxation of the Visual or Performing Artist
Texas Accountants for the Arts
1540 Sul Ross, Houston, TX 77006
713/526-4876

The Visual Artist and the Law by Paul H Epstein

What Every Artist & Collector Should Know About the Law by Scott Hodes

What Every Artist Should Know About Copyright by Vincent N Palladino
San Diego Lawyers for the Arts
Peter Karlen
205 Prospect St #400, La Jolla, CA 92037
619/454-9696

See also page 71 for publications on taxes.

Businesses, Lawyers & Accountants

Finding the Right Lawyer

Remember, it will cost you more to solve a problem than to try to prevent it in the first place. As an artist with legal questions, you don't want a lawyer who specializes in real estate or accident law, i.e. if you are working out a licensing or royalty agreement you want an "intellectual property attorney" who specializes in copyright or publishing law.

Before filing a suit, it's good to consider arbitration. Some of the organizations in this section can lead you to the right lawyer for arbitration/mediation. Also check out:

- *Local bar associations*
- *Graphic Artists Guild 212/463-7730 (free referral to members)*
- *Ask a friend*
- *Martindale-Hubbell Law Directory, lists lawyers by their area of expertise.*

It's a good idea to evaluate your lawyer's resumé—see what cases he might have worked on that might be similar to yours. Be sure you understand the lawyer's pricing structure (i.e. how much you will be charged for speaking to him for five minutes on the phone, etc.). Sometimes it's better to pay a higher per hour cost for an expert in a given area, because he takes much less time if he is knowledgeable in that area. You want to feel confident and comfortable with any lawyer you choose. Maybe you can even work out a trade of your artwork for his services.

The following are listed alphabetically by state, then city within the state.

Amy L Neiman/Lawyer
11755 Wilshire Blvd #1310, Los Angeles, CA 90025
310/575-5555
Specializes in art preservation; also works with all aspects for artists.

Arts Inc
315 W 9th St #201, Los Angeles, CA 90015
213/627-9276
Management consultation for non-profit art organizations, resources and services.

San Diego Lawyers for the Arts
Peter Karlen
205 Prospect St #400, La Jolla, CA 92037
619/454-9696
No legal services, only seminars and written information.

Support Center
8361 Vedring St #304, St, San Diego, CA 92111
619/292-5702
Teaches grant writing, computer and other business functions.

Business Arts Council
Martin Weil
465 California St 9Fl, San Francisco, CA 94104
416/392-4511 ex 866

David Comarow/Lawyer
619/482-7900
Represents artists worldwide.

California Lawyers for the Arts
Alma Robinson
Fort Mason Center Bldg C-255, San Francisco, CA 94123
415/775-7200

LTJ and Associates
1728 Union St #200, San Francisco, CA 94123
415/771-0598

Support Center
70 10th St #201, San Francisco, CA 94103
415/552-7584

Mark Jacobsen/Lawyer
137 E Anapamer St, Santa Barbara, CA 93101
805/962-3999

California Lawyers for Arts
Judith Bowman
1549 11th St #200, Santa Monica, CA 90401
310/395-8893
Has books, seminars, arts arbitration and mediation services. Call for further information/sliding pay scale.

Colorado Lawyers for Arts
200 Grant St #303 E, Denver, CO 80203
303/722-7994

James Knowlton/Lawyer
1775 Sherman St #1770, Denver, CO 80203

Connecticut Volunteer Lawyers for Art
227 Lawrence St, Hartford, CT 06106
203/566-4770

Businesses, Lawyers & Accountants

Business Volunteers for the Arts
Arts Council of Greater New Haven
70 Audubon St, New Haven, CT 06510
203/772-2788

Baker McKenzie
815 Connecticut Ave NW #900, Washington, DC 20006
202/452-7000
Largest law firm in the world, with expertise in all major areas including: publishing, copyright trademark; merchandising; entertainment and communications.

Business Volunteers for the Arts
Cultural Alliance of Greater DC
Barbara Greenfield
410 8th St NW #600, Washington, DC 20004
202/638-2406 ext 24

Volunteer Lawyers for the Arts
918 16th St NW #503, Washington, DC 20006
202/429-0229

Washington Area Lawyers for Arts/WALA
410 8th Ave NW #400, Washington, DC 20005
202/393-2826

Volunteer Lawyers for Arts Program
400 Pierce Blvd, Clearwater, FL 34616
813/464-3327

ArtServe
PO Box 4189, Ft Lauderdale, FL 33338
305/462-9191
This organization houses a business center, Lawyers for the Arts and Business Volunteers for the Arts and has many services for artists.

Business Volunteers for the Arts
150 W Flagler St #2500, Miami, FL 33130

Business Volunteers for the Arts
Beverly Losman
235 Inernational Blvd NW, PO Box 1740, Atlanta, GA 30301
404/586-8536

Volunteer Lawyers for the Arts
141 Pryor St #2030, Atlanta, GA 30303
404/525-6046

Art and Business Council
Teri Gens
55 E Monroe #1640, Chicago, IL 60603
312/372-1876

Illinois CPA Society
222 S Riverside Plaza, Chicago, IL 60606
312/993-0393

Keck, Mahin & Cate
Les Chard
312/634-7700

Lawyers for the Creative Arts/LCA
Tim Kelley
213 W Institute Pl #411, Chicago, IL 60610
312/944-2787

Left Brain Tax Services
213 W Institute Pl #308, Chicago IL
312/944-4128   708/351-8883

Patricia Felch/Lawyer
3 First National Plaza #3600, Chicago, IL 60602-4283
312/236-0404

Kansas Bar Association Committee on Arts
913/234-5696

Volunteer Lawyers for the Arts
161 North Mill St, Lexington, KY 40507
606/255-2951

Louisiana Volunteer Lawyers for Arts
821 Gravier #600, New Orleans, LA 70112
504/523-1465

Dawn M Thomas Kuzio/Lawyer
Box 76, Belfast, ME 04915
207/567-3053

Volunteer Lawyers Project
PO Box 547, Portland, ME 04112
207/774-4348

Maryland Volunteer Lawyers for Arts
218 W Saratoga St 2Fl, Baltimore, MD 21201-3538
410/752-1633

The Artists Foundation
86 Harrison Ave #309, Boston, MA 03127
617/859-3810

Businesses, Lawyers & Accountants

Volunteer Lawyers for the Arts
PO Box 8784, Boston, MA 02114
617/523-1764

Carol Spack/Lawyer
PO Box 100, Newtonville, MA 02160
617/965-9500

Carla Messman
936 Aurora Ave, St Paul, MN 55104
612/646-6343
Author of "Artist's Tax Guide." Offers financial planning, retirement plan options, estate planning and assistance from an artist's viewpoint on an hourly basis.

Midwest Center for Arts & Law
Ann Marie Thatcher
882 Kenneth St, St Paul, MN 55116
612/698-9274

Resources and Counseling for the Arts
75 W 5th St #429, St Paul, MN 55102
612/292-4381

Kansas City Attorneys for the Arts
Dale Werts
2345 Grand Ave, Kansas City, MO 64141
816/474-6460

St Louis Volunteer Lawyers and Accountants for the Arts
Sue Greenberg
3540 Washington 2Fl, St Louis, MO 63101
314/652-2410

Montana Volunteer Lawyers for the Arts
PO Box 8687, Missoula, MT 59807
406/721-1835

Business Committee on the Arts
1 Granite Pl, Concord, NH 03301
603/224-8300

Volunteer Lawyers for the Arts
Schenectady League of Arts/Douglas Pace
19 Clinton Ave, Albany, NY 12207
518/449-5380

Business Committee for the Arts
Judith Jedlicka
1775 Broadway #510, New York, NY 10019
212/664-0600

Doctors for Arts
105 W 78th St, New York, NY 10024
212/496-5172
Refers artists to specialists who have agreed to discount their fees 20%.

Foundation for the Community of Artists
280 Broadway, New York, NY 10007
Offers financial services to artists, including tax preparation, pension planning, general advice on financial management, and bookkeeping systems.

Lloyd J Jassin/Lawyer
888 7th Ave #1503, New York, NY 10106
212/489-6246
Copyright and trademark concentration.

Nancy Krinsky
718/789-6003
Tax preparation.

Russo & Burke
Joseph Burke
600 Third Ave, New York, NY 10016
212/557-9600
Works with photographers.

Volunteer Lawyers for the Arts
Dan Mayer
1 E 53rd St 6Fl, New York, NY 10022
212/319-2787

VUGG
300 E 42nd St, New York, NY 10007

Entrepreneurial Center for Small Business Development
Constance Hallinan Lagan
35 Claremont Ave, North Babylon, NY 11703
516/661-5181

Karl S Sawyer
Charlotte, NC
704/375-9181
Copyright lawyer for artists.

North Carolina Volunteer Lawyers for the Arts
PO Box 26513, Raleigh, NC 27611-6513
919/831-6234

Businesses, Lawyers & Accountants

Cincinnati Area Lawyers for Arts
ML003 Univ Cincinnati, Cincinnati OH 45221
513/475-4383

Volunteer Lawyers for the Arts
Cleveland Bar Assoc
113 St Clair Ave NE #225, Cleveland, OH 44114
216/696-3525

Toledo Volunteer Lawyers for the Arts
Arnold Gottlieb
608 Madison Ave #1523, Toledo, OH 43604
419/255-3344

Oklahoma Lawyers for the Arts
Eric King
Box 255, Oklahoma City, OK 73083
405/340-7988

Leonard DuBoff/Lawyer
12440 SW Iron Mountain Blvd, Portland, OR 97219
503/452-1228

North West Lawyers for the Arts/NWLA
Kohel Haver
330 Pacific Bldg, 520 SW Yamhill, Portland, OR 97204
503/295-2787

Community Accountants
University City Science Center/Beth Simon
3508 Market St #135, Philadelphia, PA 19104
215/662-0211

Philadelphia Volunteer Lawyers for the Arts
Dorothy Manou
251 S 18th St, Philadelphia, PA 19103
215/545-3385

Ocean State Lawyers for the Arts
David Spatt
PO Box 19, Saunderstown, RI 02874-0019
401/789-5686
Arts Entertainment law newsletter/$10 a year.

Lawyers for the Arts
South Dakota Arts Council/Shirley Sneze
230 S Philips Ave #204, Sioux Falls, SD 57102
605/367-5678

Volunteer Lawyers for the Arts
Bob Sullivan
320 6th Ave #100, Nashville, TN 37219
615/244-1713

Austin Lawyers & Accountants for the Arts
512/476-4458

Texas Lawyers for the Arts
2917 Swiss Ave, Dallas, TX 75204
214/821-2522

Business Volunteers for the Arts
Elizabeth Nelson
1 Tandy Ctr #150, Ft Worth, TX 76102
817/870-2567

Business Volunteers for the Arts
1331 Lamar #550, Houston, TX 77010
713/650-3189

Texas Accountants & Lawyers for the Arts
Jane Lowery
1540 Sul Ross, Houston, TX 77006
713/526-4876
Also has a mediation line at 800/526-TALA.

Utah Lawyers for the Arts
James Stewart
170 S Main St #1500, Salt Lake City, UT 84101
801/521-3200

Alyssa Salomon
3607 Hawthorne Ave, Richmond, VA 23222
804/321-2737
Tax and accounting services.

artTax
206/523-6064
Servicing the Seattle arts community. Professionals with nearly 20 years experience in tax planning and preparation—specifically tailored to arts practitioners.

Business Volunteers for the Arts
1301 5th Ave #2400, Seattle, WA 98101
206/389-7278

Washington Lawyers for the Arts
219 First Ave S #315-A, Seattle, WA 98104

Artists Legal Advice Services
183 Bathurst St 1 Fl, Toronto, Ontario
Canada M5T 2R7
416/360-0772
Services artists in the province of Ontario only.

CHAPTER III

GRANTS
&
RESIDENCIES

Grant Writers

One of the better places to locate a grant writer is in your local arts council's office files. If they don't have any references, try your local art newspaper. Someone from out of town can assist you too, so try the people listed below.

Artist Support Services
Susan Farner
603 Eagles Crest Village Ln #16, Roswell, GA 30076
404/640-9056

Artsource
CA Reed
PO Box 46926, Seattle, WA 98146
206/762-5525

Gail Baillergeau
510/532-7759

Genie Stelnicki
4218 N Belle, Chicago, IL 60618
312/583-3066

Grants International
Nora Lindberg
PO Box 995, Galt, CA 95632
209/745-7186

Hannah Ullman
2243 Derby, Berkeley, CA 94705
510/845-6911

Michelle Becker
212/942-4851

Seliger and Associates
800/540-8906

Foundation Libraries

These special libraries disseminate current information on foundation and corporate giving through their branch offices, as well as 200 cooperating libraries in all 50 states and abroad. Through these library collections, grantseekers have free access to core publications plus a wide range of books, periodicals and research documents relating to foundations and philanthropy. Services include reference librarians to assist visitors, free orientations, and microform and photocopying facilities.

The Foundation Center
1001 Connecticut Ave NW #938, Washington, DC 20036
202/331-1400

The Foundation Library
50 Hurt Plz #150, Atlanta, GA 03030-2914
404/880-0094

The Foundation Center
1422 Euclid Ave #1356, Cleveland, OH 44115
216/861-1934
9:30-4:30. Free grants orientation seminar.

The Foundation Center
312 Sutter St, San Francisco, CA 94108
415/397-0902
10:00-4:45.

The Foundation Center
79 5th Ave, New York, NY 10003-3076
212/620-4230
10:00-5:00. Call for complete catalog of books on grants.

New Haven Foundation Philanthropic Library
70 Audubon St 1Fl, New Haven, CT 06516
203/777-2386

Grant Writing Workshops

Contact your local arts council for seminars and workshops in your area. Sometimes the organizations listed in the previous chapter sponsor such workshops.

Cause Effective
39 W 14th St #408, New York, NY 10011
212/807-6896
Workshops for resource development of grants.

Grantsmanship Center
Susan Stanton
PO Box 17220, 1125 W 6th St 5Fl, Los Angeles, CA 90017
213/482-3622 800/842-8484
This organization holds various seminars for the individual and non-profit sector. They also have a catalog that sells books on the subject.

Illinois Assocation of Non-Profit Organizations
Ellen Dick
8 S Michigan #3000, Chicago, IL 60603
708/386-9385
Provides a variety of grant writing, bookkeeping and media seminars.

Grants & Residencies

Grant Writing Software

Patricia Rife and Associates
1139A Kauhikoa Dr, Haiku, HI 96708
808/575-9502
$59.95ppd.

Publications on Grants

*Many of these resources can be found at a Foundation Library (see previous page). Addresses and telephone numbers of publishers of books noted with an asterisk following their name can be located on pages 74-76. Titles with ** previous to title denote that ArtNetwork sells these books (916/432-7630).*

American Art Directory
RR Bowker*
Lists scholarships and fellowships.

An Artist's Resource Book
Go Far Press
1245 S Orange Dr, Los Angeles, CA 90019
213/937-6021
$16ppd

Annual Register of Grant Support
Reed Reference Publishers*

Approaching Corporations for Support: A Guide for Arts Organizations by Sarah Iley
Council for Business and the Arts in Canada*

Art & Culture Funding Report
Funding Research Council
1611 N Kent St, Arlington, VA 22209
703/528-1000
Monthly newsletter.

Art & Design Scholarships: A Complete Guide
800/977-2665
$20.95.

The Art of Winning Foundation Grants by Howard Hillman and Karin Abarbanel
Vanguard Press
424 Madison Ave, New York, NY 10017

Artsmoney: Raising It, Saving It, and Earning It by Joan Jeffri

Attorney General's Guide to Charities
Funding Information Center
800/952-5225

Catalog of Federal Domestic Assistance
Referred to as the Sears and Roebuck Catalog of federal funding.

College Blue Book: Scholarships, Fellowships, Grants and Loan
MacMillan

Corporate Giving to the Arts
American Council for the Arts*

Cultural Directory II
Lists government programs for arts.

Developing Skills in Proposal Writing by Mary Hall
Continuing Education Publications
Portland State University/Community Services
PO Box 1491, Portland, OR 97207

Directory of Computer and High Technology Grants by Andrew J Grant
Research Grant Guide
PO Box 1214, Loxahatchee, FL 33470
Lists more than 600 funding sources.

Directory of Financial Aids for Minorities

Directory of Financial Aids for Women
TGC/Reference Service Press
1100 Industrial Rd, #9, San Carlos, CA 94070
$47.50 + $4.00 shipping.

Directory of Grants in Humanities
Oryx Press
800/279-ORYX
$74.50/2,600 funding programs for the arts

Fellowships Guidebook
Art Resources International*
$8.

Foundation Directory
The Foundation Center*
Lists 7600 foundations/$140.

Foundation Fundamentals: A Guide for Grant Seekers by Carol Kurzig
The Foundation Center*

Foundation Grants Index
The Foundation Center*

Foundation Grants to Individuals edited by Lorenz Ren
The Foundation Center*

Gadney's Guide to Contests, Festivals & Grants

Get Your Money, Honey! A Student's Guide to Staying Alive
For Us Publications
PO Box 33147, Farragut Station, Washington, DC

Getting a Grant by Robert Lefferts

Grant Announcement Service
Data Inc*
A bi-weekly subscription service featuring federal, local and private grant announcements/$55 for 24 issues.

Grant Searching Simplified
Creative Resources
PO Box 2221, Asheville, NC 28802
$22.90ppd/130 pages of information, worksheets, charts.

Grants & Aids to Individual Artists
Washington International Arts Letter
$24.95.

Grants for the Arts by Virginia White

Grants Register
St Martin's Press

A Guide to Corporate Giving in the Arts by Robert A Porter

A Guide to Grants & Funding for the Individual Artist

Guidelines to Grants
Ohio Arts Council
727 E Main St, Columbus, OH 43205
614/466-2613

How To Get Money for Research by Mark Ruben
City of New York
311 E 94th St, New York, NY 10128

**Individual's Guide to Grants by Judith Margolin

Money Business: Grants and Awards for Creative Artists by Rita Roosevelt, Anita Granoff and Karen Kennedy
Artists Foundation Inc*

Money for Artists: A Guide to Grants & Awards for Individual Artists

Money for International Exchange in the Arts
American Council for the Arts*
$14.95.

**Money for Visual Artists

Money to Work - Grants for Visual Artists
Art Resources International*
107 page guide with over 80 national, regional, state and local grant opportunities with details on each and insight into the selection process/$8.00.

NAEA Scholarship Book
NAEA*
$3.00.

National Directory of Art Internships
NNAP*

National Directory of Corporate Charity by Sternberg

National Directory of Foundation Fundamentals: A Guide for Grant Seekers

National Guide to Funding in Arts and Culture
The Foundation Center*

Overview of Endowment Programs
National Endowment for the Humanities
1100 Pennsylvania Ave NW, Washington, DC 20506
202/606-8400

Program Planning and Proposal Writing by Norton J Kirtz

Proposal Writers Guide by Michael Burns
DATA Inc*

Taft Corporate Directory by Schoenthaler

Users Guide to Funding Resources

Visual Artist's Grants: A Report to the Field
Center for Arts Information*

Grants & Residencies

IRS Reporting of Grants

You may not know it, but most grants artists receive must be included in their annual tax return. Only grants that meet the following criteria are generally tax free:
- *Recipient is selected without any action on his part to enter a contest.*
- *Recipient is not required to render services as a condition to receiving the money.*
- *Amount of the award is transferred to a tax-exempt government organization.*

If you do receive a taxable grant (and try to find out before you apply), so as not to pay too much in taxes in any given grant year, see if you can split the monies received—50% in one year and 50% in the next. Additionally, for your own personal accounting, it might be best to have monthly payments transferred to your checking account (so you don't spend it all at once!) from a savings.

Grants and awards are not generally subject to the 15.3 % self-employment tax. IRS publication #520 details reporting requirements for grants. Call 800/829-1040 to have it sent to you.

Grant Givers

Send a postcard to the following list of grant givers to receive the particulars about their grants.
Some grant givers say they do not give grants to individuals. Artists have gotten around this by applying through their local arts council. Ask your arts council about this possibility.
In italics following some listings is a brief synopsis about the grants offered: deadline date(s); amount of grant; who can apply.

Ahmanson Foundation
9215 Wilshire Blvd, Beverly Hills, CA 90210

Alex J Ettle
National Sculpture Society
1177 Ave of the Americas, New York, NY 10036
212/764-5645
10/31

Alpha Kappa Alpha
Educational Advancement Foundation
5656 S Stony Island Ave, Chicago, IL 60637
312/947-0026
3/16; 5 @ $1000

American Academy in Rome
Fellowship Coordinator
7 E 60th St, New York, NY 10022-1001
212/751-7200
11/15;1 year in Rome; Painters/sculptors

Arad Arts Project
WUJS Institute
110 E 59th St, New York, NY 10022

Art Matters
Laura Donnelley
131 W 24th St, New York, NY 10011

Art Ventures Fund
Career Opportunity Grants
Jacksonville Community Foundation
112 W Adams St #1414, Jacksonville, FL 32202

Arts in General
Holly Block
79 Walker St, New York, NY 10013

Association for Visual Artists
615 Lindsay St, Chattanooga, TN 37403

Athena Foundation
Anita Contini, PO Box 6259, Long Island City, NY 11106

Barbara Deming Fund
Anita Page
PO Box 40-1043, Brooklyn, NY 11240

Bronx Council on the Arts
1738 Hone Ave, Bronx, NY 10461

Camargo Foundation
PO Box 32, E Haddam, CT 06423-0032

Capp Street Project
270 14th St, San Francisco, CA 94103

Change Inc
Denise LeBeau
PO Box 705, New York, NY 10276
212/473-3742

Ruth Chenven Foundation
7 Park Ave #103, New York, NY 10016

Cintas Fellowship
809 United Nations Plaza, New York, NY 10017-3580
212/984-5370

City Arts
1650 Arch St 19Fl, Philadelphia, PA 19103

Djerassi Foundation Resident
Artist Program
2325 Bear Gulch Rd, Woodside, CA 94062
415/852-8395

Elizabeth Foundation
PO Box 2670, New York, NY 10036

Ferguson Award
Ansel Adams Center
250 Fourth St, San Francisco, CA 94103

Fleischacker Foundation
Christine Ebel
1 Maritime Plaza #830, San Francisco, CA
94111

Florsheim Art Fund
U of South Fl/August Freundlich
PO Box 3033, Tampa, FL 33620-3033

Frances Hook Scholarship Program
430B W County Rd D, New Brighton, MN 55112
708/673-2787

Goebel Canada
Marcel Brandstat
120 Danforth Rd, Toronto, Ontario Canada
*Offers an annual international award of $25,000
for porcelain sculpture.*

Gottlieb Foundation
380 W Broadway, New York, NY 10012

Guggenheim Memorial Foundation
Robert Lindsay
90 Park Ave, New York, NY 10016

Harriet Hale Woolley Scholarships
Fondation des Etats Unis
15 Blvd Jourdan, 75690 Paris Cedex 14 France
1/31; $8000

J Paul Getty Trust Fund for Visual Arts
606 S Olive St #2400, Los Angeles, CA
90014
213/413-4042
Only artists living in Los Angeles County.

Jerome Foundation
Cynthia Gehrig
332 Minnesota St, St Paul, MN 55101
612/224-9431

John and Anna Lee Stacey
PO Box 3189, Los Angeles, CA 90051

Kate Neal Kinely Memorial Fellowship
College of Fine and Applied Arts
110 Architecture Bldg/608 E Lorado, Taft Dr,
Champaign, IL 61820
3/15; All media; 2 @ $7000

Ludwig Vogelstein Foundation
Frances Pishny
PO Box 4924, Brooklyn, NY 11240

MacArthur Foundation
140 S Dearborn St, Chicago, IL 60603

Marie Walsh Sharpe Art Foundation
711 N Tejon St #B, Colorado Springs, CO
80903

Marwen Foundation
325 W Huron #215, Chicago, IL 60610

NEA
110 Pennsylvania Ave NW #729, Washington,
DC 20506
202/682-5448

NY Foundation for the Arts
155 Ave of the Americas, New York, NY 10013

New York State Council on the Arts
Public Information Office
915 Broadway, New York, NY 10010

Pollock-Krasner Foundation
725 Park Ave, New York, NY 10021

Southeastern Center for Contemporary Art
Jeff Fleming
750 Marguerite Dr, Winston-Salem, NC
27106
910/725-1904
Private grants.

Thanks Be to Grandmother
PO Box 1449, Wainscott, NY 11975

Virginia A Groot Foundation
PO Box 1050, Evanston, IL 60204-1050
3/1; Ceramics/sculpture; $25,000

Warren Tanner Memorial Art Fund
19 Hudson St #402, New York, NY 10013

Grants & Residencies

WESTAF
1112 16th St NW #620, Washington, DC
20036

Internships

Look in the back of your art newsletters and magazines for current listings. ArtWorld Hotline (available through ArtNetwork at 916/432-7630) lists various internships available throughout the year. Many arts councils and museums sponsor internships. Sometimes college credit is possible. Most internships do not pay, although some pay very well.

National Directory of Art Internships
800/321-4510 212/223-2787

Publications on Residencies

Addresses and telephone numbers of publishers of books noted with an asterisk following their name can be located in the section "Art Business Book Publishers." Titles with ** previous to title denote that ArtNetwork sells these books (916/432-7630).

Art Colonies
Center for Arts Information*
Detailed information about mechanics of a residency.

Artists Live/Work Spaces: Changing Public Policy
415/775-7200

Residencies at National Parks
Lowertown Lofts Arts Coop/Bonnie Fournier
PO Box 65552, St Paul, MN 55165-0522
$12.50ppd.

Special Space: A Guide to Artists' Housing and Loft Living

Visual Artists Residencies: Sponsor Organizations
Mid-Atlantic Arts Foundation
11 E Chase St #2A, Baltimore, MD 21202
410/539-6656
$20ppd.

Residencies

In italics after some of the listings is information noted in the following order: dates of application; length of stays; media they accept; cost. Call or write for detailed information.

ACTS Institute/Act 1
Mr. Norman
PO Box 10153, Kansas City, MO 64111
816/753-0208
All year; 1-4 weeks; All media

Alaska Residencies
Island Institute
Box 2420, Sitka, AK 99835
907/747-3794

Alden B Dow Creativity Center
Carol Coppage
Northwood Institute, Midland, MI 48640

Archie Bray Foundation
2915 Country Club Ave, Helena, MT 59001
406/443-3502
5/15; 1 year

Arrowmont School of Arts & Crafts
PO Box 567, Gatlinburg, TN 37738

Art Barn
695 N 400 E, Valparaiso, IN 46383

Artists Workspace
Joan Kleinhans
PO Box 338, Woodstock, NY 12498

ArtPark
Joan McDonough
Box 371, Lewiston, NY 14072-0371
2-6 weeks; All media; Are paid!

Atlantic Center for the Arts
1414 Art Center Ave, New Smyrna Beach, FL 32168
904/427-6975
5-6 weeks; Scholarships available

Banff Centre for the Arts
Leighton Artist Colony, Box 1020, Banff,
Alberta Canada T0L 0C0
3x annually; 1 week-3 months

Bellagio Study Center
Rockefeller Foundation
1133 Ave of the Americas, New York, NY
10036
4-5 weeks

Bemis Foundation
614 S 11th St, Omaha, NE 68102
402/341-7130
3/1; 3-6 months; All media; Paid

Bernheim Arboretum
Charles McClure
Hwy 245, General Delivery, Clermont, KY
40110
10/15 & 12/15; Up to 4 months; Pd $2500

Blue Mountain Center
Blue Mountain Lake, NY 12812
518/352-7391
4 weeks; All media; Free

Centrum Foundation
PO Box 1158, Ft Worden State Park,
Townsend, WA 98368
206/385-3102
4/1, 10/1; 1 month; All media

Cite International Des Artes
18 rue d l'hotel de ville, 75004, Paris, France
April/Nov; 1 year in Paris; All media

Clearing
PO Box 65, Ellison Bay, WI 54210
414/854-4088
May-Oct

Contemporary Artists Center
The Beaver Mill
189 Beaver St, N Adams, MA 01247
413/663-9555

Cummington Center
Lauren K Davis
PO Box 70, Cummington, MA 01026
4/1; 2 weeks - 3 months; All media

Depot Outreach
506 W Michigan St, Duluth, MN 55802
218/727-8025
3/2; 2 weeks; All; Pd $130 per day

Dieu Donne Papermill
Mina Takahashi
3 Crosby St, 5 Fl, New York, NY 10013
212/226-0573
12/31; 5-10 days; Hand made paper; Free materials and honorarium

Dillmans Sand Lake Lodge
PO Box 98, Lac due Flambeau, WI 54538
800/359-2511
Scholarships/also holds seminars and workshops

Djerassi Foundation
2325 Bear Gulch Rd, Woodside, CA 94062
415/851-8395
3/31; 2-6 months; All media

Doghaven Center for the Arts
PO Box 283, Three Oaks, MI 49128
312/733-2246
All year; 2 months

Dorland Mountain Colony
Admissions Committee
PO Box 6, Temecula, CA 92930
3/1 and 9/1; 1-3 months; All media; $150 per month + food

Druid Heights Artist Retreat
Marcelina Martin
PO Box 697, Pt Reyes St, CA 94956
415/663-8446
1/2-3/15; 1-3 months; All media; No CA/NM

Edward Albee Foundation
Flanagan Memorial Center
14 Harrison St, New York, NY 10013
212/226-2020
1/1-4/15; 1 month; Painters

Fine Arts Work Center
24 Pearl St, Box 565, Provincetown, MA
02657
508/487-9960
2/1; 7 months; All media except film and video; $275 week stipend

Francis J Greenburger Foundation
Chris Nelson
55 Fifth Ave, New York, NY 10003
212/206-6000

Grand Marais Art Colony
Box 626, Grand Marais, MN 55604
218/387-2737

Grants & Residencies

Griffis Art Center
Artist-in-Residence
33 Granite St #103, New London, CT 06320
203/447-3431
1/15; 9/15 -6/15 9 months

Hambridge Center
Judy Barber
PO Box 339, Rabun Gap, GA 30568
March; 2 weeks - 2 months; All media

Helene Wurlitzer Foundation
HA Sauerwein
PO Box 545, Taos, NM 87871
505/758-2413
1-3 months

Hillwood Art Museum
Project Residencies/Long Island U
CW Post Campus, Brookville, NY 11548

Horizons
374 Old Montague Rd, Amherst, MA 01002
413/665-0300
3-6 weeks; Crafts; Scholarships

Idyllwild Arts Foundation
PO Box 38, Idyllwild, CA 92349

Jerome Stone Foundation
St Johns Potter
Box 6377, Collegeville, MN 56321
Stone & ceramics

Kalani Honua Oceanside Retreat
Richard Koob
RR 2 Box 4500, Pahoa-Kamaili, HI 96778

Lakeside Center for the Arts
9129 Golf Rd, Lakeside, MI 49116
616/469-1377

Lightwork
Artist in Residence/Jeffrey Hoone
316 Waverly Ave, Syracuse, NY 13244
315/443-1300
Photography; $1200 stipend and apartment

Lila Wallace-Readers Digest International Artists
Arts International
809 UN Plaza, New York, NY 10017
212/984-5370
1/17; 3-6 months; All media; Paid

MacDowell Colony
Admissions Office
100 High St, Peterborough, NH 03458
603/924-3886
1/15, 4/15, 9/15; Up to 8 weeks; All media; Small donation

Mid-Atlantic Arts Foundation
11 E Chase St #21, Baltimore, MD 21202
410/539-6656

Millay Colony for the Arts
Steepletop
PO Box 3, Austerlitz, NY 12017-0003
518/392-3103
2/1, 5/1, 9/1; 1 month; All media; Free

Montalvo Center for the Arts
Lori Wood
PO Box 158, Saratoga, CA 95071-0158
408/741-3421
3/1, 9/1; 1-3 months; All media

Morgan Mountain Art Retreat
2112 S Helen St, Melbourne, FL 32901

National Foundation for Advancement of the Arts
3915 Biscayne Blvd, Miami, FL 33137

North Carolina Arts Council
Visiting Artist Residency
Dept of Cultural Resources, Raleigh, NC
27601-2807
919/733-7897
1/15; 6-12 months; Sculptors; Paid $17,000-$25,000

New York Mills Art Retreat
RR 1 Box 217, New York Mills, MN 56567
218/385-3339
2-8 weeks; All

Nexus Press
535 Means St, Atlanta, GA 30318
404/577-3579
4/15; 1 month; Printmaking and book arts; $1000 stipend

NISDA
Box 958, Nantucket, MA 02554

Northwood Institute
Alden B Dow Center, Midland, MI 48640
517/837-4478
12/31; 10 weeks; All media; Modest stipend

Ox-Bow Workshop for the Arts
School of Art Institute of Chicago
37 S Wabash Ave #707, Chicago, IL 60603
312/899-5130
1-2 weeks

Palenville Interart Colony
PO Box 59, Palenville, NY 12463

Peace Abbey
Lewis Randa
2 N Mason St, Sherborn, MA 01770

Ragdale Foundation
Sylvia Brown
1260 N Green Bay Rd, Lake Forest, IL 60045
*1/15, 4/15, 9/15; 2 wks - 2 months; $10 per day/
scholarships available*

Ritz Carlton Artist in Residence
Michelle Payer
1 Ritz Carlton Dr, Kapalua, Maui 96761

Rocky Mountain Women's Institute
Cheryl Bezio-Gorham
7150 Montview Blvd, Denver, CO 80220

Roswell Museum and Art Center
Artist in Residence Program
100 W 11th St, Roswell, NM 88201
505/624-6744
6 month/1 yr; All media

Sas Colby
Box 6129 NDCBU, Taos, NM 87571
505/751-3667 505/751-2179

Sculpture Space Inc
Sylvia de Swaan
12 Gates St, Utica, NY 13502
315/724-8381
12/15; Up to 3 months; Sculpture

Skowhagen School of Painting and Sculpture
200 Park Ave S #1116, New York, NY 10003
212/529-0505
9 weeks

Snug Harbor Cultural Center
1000 Richmond Ter, Staten Island, NY 10301
718/448-2500
3-6 months duration

Split Rock Arts Program
U of MN
306 Westbrook Hall/77 Pleasant St SE,
Minneapolis, MN 55455

Stone Quarry Hill Art Park
Carol Jeschke
3883 Stone Quarry Rd, Cazenovia, NY 13035
315/655-3196

Studio Museum in Harlem
Director of Education
144 W 12th St, New York, NY 10027

Triangle Artists Workshop
110 Greene St #8R, New York, NY 10012
212/206-6195
3/1; 2 weeks; Painters/sculptors; $400

Ucross Foundation
2836 US Highway 14-16 E, Clearmont, WY
82835-9712
307/737-2291
*3/1, 10/1; 2 weeks-4 months; All media; Room
and board provided*

US Dept of Interior
National Park Service
PO Box 168, Yellowstone, WY 82190

Vermont Studio Center
Susan Kowalsky
PO Box 613, Johnson, VT 05656
802/635-2727
2-4 weeks; All media

Virginia Center for Creative Arts
Karen Kimble
Box VCCA, Sweet Briar, VA 24595
804/946-7236
2/1; 1 week - 3 months; Painters/sculptors

Weir Farm Heritage
735 Nod Hill Rd, Wilton, CT 06897
203/761-9945

Woodstock Artists Association
Jane Burr
28 Tinker St, Woodstock, NY 12498

Yaddo Estate
Admissions Committee
Box 395, Saratoga Spings, NY 12866
518/584-0746
1/15, 8/1; 1-2 months; All media; $20 per day

Yellow Springs Institute
John Clauser
1645 Art School Rd, Chester Springs, PA
19425
610/827-9111
11/15; 2-3 weeks

CHAPTER IV

CATALOGS & MAGAZINES

Art Supply Catalogs

Following is a list of catalogs from which artists can order supplies, books, and other useful items. Many of the companies offer specialty items as well as discounted prices on certain products. Call or send a postcard requesting a catalog. Sometimes there is a fee for a catalog, but you can usually apply that fee towards your first purchase.

AJ Friedman Art Supplies
25 W 45th St, New York, NY 10036

Andy's Art Supplies Inc
208 W 23rd St, New York, NY 10011
800/709-9600 212/675-9499

Art Carousel
Route 1, Box 16B, Walnut Shade, MI 65771

Art Express
PO Box 21662, Columbia, SC 29221
800/535-5908

Art N' Craft Supply
PO Box 5070, Slidell, LA 70469
800/642-1062

Art Production
6820 Orangethorpe Ave #H, Buena Park, CA 90620

Art Supplies Wholesale
4 Enon St Rt 1A, N Beverly, MA 01915

Art Supply Warehouse
360 Main Ave, Norwalk, CT 06851
800/243-5038

Artgrafix
15 Tech Cir, Natick, MA 01760
800/443-4421

Arthur Brown
2 W 46th St, New York, NY 10036-4502
800/237-0619

Artisans/Santa Fe Inc
Paul Bell
717 Canyon Rd, Santa Fe, NM 87501
800/331-6375 505/908-2179

Artist Supply
415 Forest Ave, Portland, ME 04101
800/876-8076

Artists' Connection
600 Rt 1 S, Iselin, NJ 08830
800/851-9333

B R Artcraft Co
6701 Cherry Hill Rd, Baldwin, MD 21013

Charrette Corp
31 Olympia Ave, Woburn, MA 01888
617/935-6000

Cheap Joe's Art Stuff
374 Industrial Park, Boone, NC 28607
800/227-2788

Co-Op Artists' Materials
205 Armour Dr NE, Atlanta, GA 30324
800/877-3242

Crest Art
205 Armour Dr, Atlanta, GA 30324

Daler-Rowney
2 Corporation Dr, Cranbury, NJ 08512
609/655-5252

Daniel Smith
4150 First Avenue S, Seattle, WA 98134
800/426-6740 206/223-9599

Dick Blick Co
Highway 150 E, PO Box 1267,Galesburg, IL 61401
309/343-6181

Dixie Art Supplies
2612 Jefferson Hwy, New Orleans, LA 70121

Dynamic Graphics
PO Box 1901, Peoria, IL 61656-1901
800/255-8800

Eastern Arts Connection
38 Pine Dr, Farmington, CT 06085
203/673-6243

Enterprise Art
2860 Roosevelt Blvd, Clearwater, FL 33520

Flax Artist Materials
1699 Market St, San Francisco, CA 94103
800/547-7778

Grand Central Artists Materials
14 E 41st St, New York, NY 10017
212/679-0023

Catalogs & Magazines

Art Supply Catalogs (cont.)

Graphic Arts Bookstore Catalog
1730 N Lynn St, Arlington, VA 22209

Grumbacher Art
30 Englehard Dr, Cranbury, NJ 08512

Italian Book Store
40 W Ray Burn, PO Box 300, Millington, NJ 07946

Jerry's Artarama
PO Box 1105, New Hyde Park, NY 11040
800/U-ARTIST

Joe Kubert Art Supplies
37 Myrtle Ave, Dover, NJ 07801
201/361-1327

John Pike Art Products
607/754-1761

Nasco Arts & Crafts
901 Janesville Ave, Ft Atkinson, WI 53538
800/557-9595 414/563-2446

New York Central Supply Co
62 Third Ave, New York, NY 10003
212/473-7705

Orange Art
PO Box 213, Woodstock, CT 06281
800/253-8975

Ott's Art Supply
102 Hungate Dr, Greenville, NC 27858
800/356-3289

Pearl Paint Co
800/221-6845

Perma Colors
226 E Tremont, Charlotte, NC 28203
704/333-9201

Pitman Art Supply
109 Market Pl, Glassboro, NJ 08028
609/881-9119

Pyramid Art Supply
923 Hickory Ln, PO Box 8104, Mansfield, OH 44901
800/637-0955

Red Rose Gallerie
PO Box 1859, Burlingame, CA 94011

Rex Art
2263 SW 37th Ave, Miami, FL 33145
305/445-1413

Rubars
1066 47th Ave #1, Oakland, CA 94601

S&S Worldwide
75 Mill St, Colchester, CT 06415
203/537-3451

Sax Arts & Crafts
PO Box 51710, New Berlin, WI 53151
414/784-6880

South Street Art Supply
515 Spring Garden St, Philadelphia, PA 19123

Stacor
285 Emmet St, Newark, NJ 07114
800/782-2677

Stu-Art Supplies
2045 Grand Ave, Baldwin, NY 11510
516/546-5151

Texas Art Supply
2001 Montrose Blvd, Houston, TX 77006
800/888-9278 713-526-5221

Tools of the Trade
PO Box 23556, Lexington, KY 40526
606/223-3438

Triangle Art Center
PO Box 8079, Princeton, NJ 08543
609/883-3600

United Art Education Supply
Box 9219, Ft Wayne, IN 46899
800/322-3247

Utrecht Manufacturing Co
33-35 St, Brooklyn, NY 11232
718/768-2525

Visual Systems
1596 Rockville Pike, Rockville, MD 20852

White Mountain Art Supply
800/321-9002

Ziegler Art Supply
PO Box 50037, Tulsa, OK 74150

Art Magazines

It is important to keep current on what is happening in the artworld. These publications, covering different topics and various areas of the country, will help you do just that.
Request a "review copy and rate card" on your business letterhead. Asking for a rate card indicates to the magazine that you are interested in advertising, and thus they will often send you a complimentary copy. You probably are not interested in advertising, however!) Write for five magazines a week, read them, and soon you will be an expert in your field!

510 News
PO Box 3994, Berkeley, CA 94703

African Arts
John Povey
405 Hilgard Ave, Los Angeles, CA 90024
213/825-1218

Airbrush Action
Clifford Stieglitz
PO Box 2052, Lakewood, NJ 08701
908/364-2111

Airbrush Magazine
Mickey Harris
3676 Cosby Hwy, Cosby, TN 37722

Alabama Arts
1 Dexter Ave, Montgomery, AL 36130

American Art Journal
Jan Turano
730 5th Ave, New York, NY 10019
212/541-9600

American Art Review
Tom Kellaway
Box 480500, Kansas City, MO 64148

American Artist
Stephen Doherty
PO Box 1213, Newark, NJ 07101-1213

American Arts Quarterly
PO Box 1654 Cooper Station, New York, NY 10276
212/260-0176

American Indian Arts
Roanne Goldfein
7314 E Osborn Dr, Scottsdale, AZ 85251
602/994-5445

Applied Arts
Peter Giffen
885 Don Mills #324, Toronto, Ontario
Canada M3C 1V9

Art Access
Debbi Lester
621 Western Ave #E, Seattle, WA 98104
206/467-4167

Art & Antiques
3 E 54th St 11Fl, New York, NY 10022
212/752-5557

Art & Artists
Elliott Barowitz
280 Broadway #412, New York, NY 10007

Art and Asia Pacific
Dinah Dysart
PO Box 480, Roseville, Sydney NSW
2069 Australia

Art & Auction
Amy Page
440 Park Ave S 14Fl, New York, NY 10016
212/479-9555

Art & Design News
Jean Pulliam
5783 Park Plaza Ct, Indianapolis, IN 46220
317/849-6110

Art & Framing
Ed Warkentin
109 - 12 K de K Ct, N Westminster, BC
Canada V3M 6C5

Art Beat
Kathleen King
PO Box 123, Mt Shasta, CA 96067

Art Brokerage
Donna Rose
PO Box 3730, Ketchum, ID 83340
208/726-0193

Art Brut
Kathy Vlako
1625 Beechwood Blvd, Pittsburgh, PA 15217

Catalogs & Magazines

Art Magazines (cont.)

Art Business News
Carol King
19 Old Kings Hwy, Darien, CT 06820
800/346-0085

Art Calendar
Carolyn Blakeslee
PO Box 199, Upper Fairmount, MD 21867
410/651-9150

Art Collectors Quarterly
Elaine Kwan
860 Cedar Ln, Northbrook, IL 60062

Art Das Kunstmagazin
Postfach 30 20 40, 2000 Hamburg 36,
Germany 20560

Art Gallery of Ontario
Clara Hargittay
317 Dundas St W, Toronto, Ontario Canada
M5T 1G4
416/977-0414

Art Guide Northwest
13205 9th Ave NW, Seattle, WA 98177
206/367-6831

Art Impressions
Yvonne Sheppard
344 Edgeley Blvd, Concord, Ontario Canada
L4K 4B7
905/738-2310

Art In America
575 Broadway, New York, NY 10012
212/941-2800

Art In Wisconsin
3115 S Superior St, Milwaukee, WI 53207

Art International
M Peppiatt
77 Rue des Archives, Paris 75003 France

Art Issues
8721 Santa Monica Blvd #6, Los Angeles, CA
90069
213/876-4508

Art Journal
Jane Edelson
275 7th Ave, 5Fl, New York, NY 10001

Art Life
PO Box 36777, Tucson, AZ 85740

Art Magazine of Modern Artists
Wu Yingqi
109 Huan Jiaoping 630053, Chong Qing PR
China

Art Marketing Letter
140 Point Judith Rd #C, Narragansett, RI
02882-3451

Art Muscle
Debra Brehmer
901 W National Ave, Milwaukee, WI 53204
414/672-8485

Art New England
Carla Munsat
425 Washington St, Brighton, MA 02135
617/782-3008

Art Nexus
8877 Collins Ave #809, Surfside, FL 33154

Art Northwest
1157 NE Malheur Ave, Roseburg, OR 97470

Art Now
97 Grayrock Rd, PO Box 5541, Clinton, NJ
08809-5541
908/638-5255

The Art of Self Promotion
Ilise Benun
302 Garden St, Hoboken, NJ 07030
201/653-0783

Art of the West
Vicki Stavig
15612 Highway 7 #235, Minnetonka, MN
55345
612/935-5850

Art Papers
Glenn Harper
PO Box 77348, Atlanta, GA 30357
404/588-1837

Art Students League News
Lawrence Campbell
215 West 57th St, New York, NY 10019
212/247-4510

Art Talk
Chris Smith
PO Box 8508, Scottsdale, AZ 85252

Art Tech News
Vital Fact Co
EM Jones
9507 Ashworth Ave N, Seattle, WA 98103

Art Therapy
Gary Barlow
1202 Allanson Rd, Mundelein, IL 60060
708/949-6064

Art Times
Cornelia Seckel
PO Box 730, Mt Marion, NY 12456
914/246-6944

ArtBeat
Outlook
PO Box 1938, Ft Bragg, CA 95468

Arte
via Cadore 19, 20135 Milano, Italia

ARTE
Donnell Brown
PO Box 190922, Dallas, TX 75219-0922
214/351-0835

ARTFBI
Jeffrey Gates
PO Box 2769, Silver Springs, MD 20915
301/949-0436

ArtForum
John Gould
PO Box 423, Moorhead, MN 56560
218/233-6676

Artforum
Ingrid Sischy
65 Bleecker Street, New York, NY 10012
212/475-4000

Artisan's Commonwealth
Stephen Clerico
PO Box 192, Free Union, VA 22940

Artist Resource Newsletter
1695 W 2nd Ave, Vancouver, BC Canada
V6J 1H3

Artist Trust
Mayumi Tsustakawa
1402 3rd Ave #404, Seattle, WA 98101
206/467-8734

Artists
Rada Petrovic
188-194 York Wy, London N7 9QR England

Artists Alliance Inc
1513 E 8th Ave, Tampa, FL 33605-3707

Artist's Magazine
Greg Sharpless
1507 Dana Ave, Cincinnati, OH 45207
800/283-0963

Artist's Resources Letter
Career Services Office
230 The Fenway, Boston, MA 02115

Artists Update
1200 Sixth Ave, Detroit, MI 48226-2461

Artletter
Susan Anderson
10206 Penn Ave S, Bloomington, MN 55431

ARTnews
Grace L Scalera
48 West 38th St 9Fl, New York, NY 10018
212/398-1690

ArtNewsletter
Bonnie Barrett Stretch
48 West 38th St 9Fl, New York, NY 10018
212/398-1690

Arts & Activities
Leven C Leatherbury
591 Camino de la Reina #200, San Diego,
CA 92108

Arts Atlantic
Joseph Sherman
PO Box 848, Charlottestown, Prince Edward
Island, Canada C1A 7L9

Arts Etc
Terese Newman
PO Box 4189, Killingsworth, CT 06147

Catalogs & Magazines

Art Magazines (cont.)

Arts Indiana
Lucie Aytes
47 S Pennsylvania St #701, Indianapolis, IN
46204-3622
317/632-7894

Arts Newsletter
Sharon Morgan
PO Box 1315, Newport, OR 97365

Arts Review
69 Faroe Rd, London England W14 OEL

Arts Review
John Casey
1269 First St #4, Sarasota, FL 34236
813/364-5825

Arts Review
Wes Walls
110 Mabel Dodge Ln, PO Box 2896,
Taos, NM 87571

Arts Wire
Anne Focke
811 1st Ave, Colman Bldg #403, Seattle, WA
98104

ArtScene
Thomas Brossart
PO Box 619, Sedona, AZ 86339

Artscene
PO Box 861176, Los Angeles, CA 90086
213/482-4724

Artsletter
800 10th St #2, Sacramento, CA 95814

ArtSource Quarterly
ArtNetwork
PO Box 1268, 18757 Wildflower Dr,
Penn Valley, CA 95946
916/432-7630
Guide to marketing art.

Artspace
727 East Main St, Columbus, OH 43205

Artspeak
Margot Palmer-Poroner
245 8th Ave #285, New York, NY 10011
212/398-1690

Artsplace
PO Box 2506, Knoxville, TN 37901

ARTtalk
75 Liberty St, Beacon, NY 12508

Artweek
Kitty Spaulding
2149 Paragon Dr #100, San Jose, CA 95131
800/733-2916 408/441-7065

ARTwork
Teller Thomas
1837 Divisadero, San Francisco, CA 94115

ArtWorld Hotline
ArtNetwork
PO Box 1268, 18757 Wildflower Dr,
Penn Valley, CA 95946
916/432-7630
Monthly leads to artworld sales.

Asian Artist Forum
Joyce Nako
1279 1/2 Muirfield Rd, Los Angeles, CA
90019

AsianArtNews
Ian Findlay-Brown
Gleanealy Mansion #2A, 7 Glenealy,
Central Hong Kong

Aspiring Cartoonist
PO Box 18679, Indianapolis, IN 46218

Aviation Art
Michael O'Leary
7950 Deering Ave, Canoga Park, CA 91304
818/887-0550

BCA News
1775 Broadway, New York, NY 10019

Bomb
Betty Sussler
594 Broadway #1002A, New York, NY
10012
212/431-3943

Book Arts
Page Two
PO Box 77167, Washington, DC 20013
800/821-6604

Buckeye Artisan
PO Box 954, Westerville, OH 43081
614/895-1663

CAA Newsletter
Susan Ball
275 Seventh Ave, New York, NY 10001

Canadian Art
Wendy Ingram
70 The Esplanade 4Fl, Toronto, Ontario
Canada M5E 1R2
416/368-8854

Caribe Magazine
Marta Vega
408 W 58th St, New York, NY 10019
212/307-7420

Chicago Gallery News
Natalie van Straaten
730 N Franklin #308, Chicago, IL 60610
312/649-0064

Collector Prints Old and New
Books Americana/Carl Luckey
PO Box 2326, Florence, AL 35630

Colorado Arts
Ted Pinkowitz
200 Grant St #303D, Denver, CO
80203-4020

Communication Arts
Jean Coyne
PO Box 10300, 410 Sherman Ave, Palo Alto,
CA 94303
415/326-6040

Competitions
G Stanley Collyer
PO Box 20445, Louisville, KY 40250

Computer Artist
Jan Hoirner
10 Tara Blvd 5Fl, Nashua, NH 03062

Corporate Art News
Richard Walker
48 West 38th St 9Fl, New York, NY 10018
212/398-1690

Correo del Arte Hispano
150 W 58th St, New York, NY 10019

Creative Ohio
Dodie Melvin
4057 Wall St, Centerburg, OH 43011

Curator
PO Box 3000, Denville, NJ 07834

The Cutting Edge
Box 826, Island Lake, IL 60042
708/526-0030
Framing tips.

Deadlines
17 W Hawley Rd, Hawley, MA 01339

Decor
Larry Allbright
330 N 4th St, St Louis, MO 63102
314/421-5445
Has an annual source directory.

Design Notes
Art of Design Center
PO Box 2223, Lewisburg, TN 37091

Design Spirit
Suzanne Koblentz-Goodman
438 Third St, Brooklyn, NY 11215

Detroit Focus
Vincent Carducci
PO Box 32823, Detroit, MI 48232-0823

Dialogue
PO Box 2572, Columbus, OH 43216
614/621-3704

Digest
Joseph Mehan
PO Box 155, New Britain, CT 06050

Electronic Link
Peter Giffen
885 Don Mills Rd #324, Don Mills, Ontario
Canada M3C 1V9
416/510-0909

Equine Art
PO Box 1315, Middleburg, VA 22117

Catalogs & Magazines

Art Magazines (cont.)

Equine Images
Carole Butler
PO Box 916, Fort Dodge, IA 50501

Federation of Modern Painters and Sculptors
Haim Mendelson
234 W 21 St, New York, NY 10011

Fiber Network
Julie Berner
PO Box 10007, Eugene, OR 97440

Fiberarts
Mary Orban
50 College St, Asheville, NC 28801
704/253-0467

Flash Art
799 Broadway #226, New York, NY 10003
212/477-4905

Forum Arts
7 Highland Parkway, Rochester, NY14620

Galerias en Galerias
1 Herald Plaza, Miami, FL 33132

Galeries Magazine
88 rue Saint-Martin, 75004 Paris, France

Graphic Design: USA
Susan Benson
1556 3rd Ave #405, New York, NY 10128

Greetings
Mackay Publishing/Milton Kristt
307 Fifth Ave, New York, NY 10015
212/679-6677

HOW
Laurel Harper
1507 Dana Ave, Cincinnati, OH 45207
513/531-2222

Illustrator
Don Jardine
500 S 4th St, Minneapolis, MN 55415

Informart
1727 E Second St, Casper, WY 82601
307/237-1659

Inside Art
Stephen Parks
PO Box 181, Embudo, NM 87531

Inside Story
Columbia County Council on the Arts
PO Box 461, Philmont, NY 12565

Journal of Aesthetics & Art Criticism
Donald Crawford
114 N Murray St, Madison, WI 53715
608/262-5839

Journal of the Print World
1000 Winona Rd, Meredith, NH 03253

KOAN
PO Box 6096, Silver Springs, MD 20916
301/871-8208

L'Art Plein Cadre
Dominique Bosch
67 Rue Provence, 75009 Paris, France

Latin American Art
Michael Marcellino
7824 E Lewis Ave, Scottsdale, AZ 85257
602/947-8423

Local Arts
2208 N Flower St, Santa Ana, CA 92706
714/285-9655

Manhattan Arts
Renee Phillips
200 E 72 St #26-L, New York, NY 10021
212/472-1660

Master Drawing Newsletter
Susan Mathisen
33 E 36 St, New York, NY 10016

Modern Painters
Fred Stern
44 Paulin Blvd, Leonia, NJ 07605

Museum News
Bill Anderson
1225 Eye St NW #200, Washington, DC 20005
202/289-1818

Museum Store Magazine
Dixie Griffin
501 S Cherry St #460, Denver, CO 80222

Museums New York
448 W 51st St GrFl , New York, NY 10019

New Art Examiner
Janet Magnesun
314 W Institute Pl, Chicago, IL 60610
312/649-9900

New Collage Magazine
5700 N Tamiani Tr, Sarasota, FL 33580

News & Views
NAMTA/Hope Crawley
178 Lakeview Ave, Clifton, NJ 07011
201/546-6400

The Newsletter
Caroll Michels
491 Broadway, New York, NY 10012

October
225 Lafayette St #1012, New York, NY 10012
212/343-0798

Office Museum Directory
3004 Glenview Rd, Wilmette, IL 60091

Official Print Guide
Ruth M Pollard/House of Collectibles
201 E 50th St, New York, NY 10022

On The Wing
James Leitzell
200 P St #C12, Sacramento, CA 95814

Options!
Pardus Inc
28 Moya Lp, Santa Fe, NM 87505
505/466-9824

Pacific Art & Travel
Cindy Nobriga
430 Hookahi St #23, Wailuku, Maui HI 96793

Palette Talk
30 Englehard Dr, Cranbury, NJ 08512

Previews
Tom Oliphant
PO Box 569, Sedona, AZ 86336

Print
Martin Fox
3200 Tower Oaks Blvd, Rockville, MD 20852
212/463-0600

Print Collector's Newsletter
Jacqueline Brody
119 E 79th St, New York, NY 10021
212/988-5959

Public Art Review
Bruce Wright
2324 University Ave W #102, Minneapolis,
MN 55114-1802

Reflex
Loch Adamson
105 S Main #204, Seattle, WA 98104
206/682-7688

Revue
Jan McNutt
302 W 13th St, Loveland, CO 80537

San Diego Arts Monthly
Randy Caler
PO Box 16773, San Diego, CA 92176-6773
619/239-0511

San Francisco Arts Monthly
Elizabeth Crabtree
655 Bryant St, San Francisco, CA 94107-1612

Sculpture Maquette
1050 17th St NW #250, Washington, DC
20036
202/785-1144

Short Subjects
Philadelphia Cultural Alliance
320 Walnut St 5Fl, Philadelphia, PA 19106

The Silkworm
Anne Sendgikoski
12213 Distribution Wy, Beltsville, MD 20705
301/595-0550

South East Arts
10 Mount Ephraim, Tunbridge Wells, Kent
TN4 8AS England

Southwest Art
Susan McGarry
PO Box 460535, Houston, TX 77056
713/850-0990

Catalogs & Magazines

Art Magazines (cont.)

Step-by-Step Graphics
John Fennell
6000 N Forest Park Dr, Peoria, IL 61614

Sunshine Artists
422 W Fairbanks Ave #300, Winter Park, FL 32789
407/539-3939

Sunstorm
Victor Forbes
1014 Drew Ct, Ronkonkoma, NY 11779

US Art
Lynda Holker
220 S 6th St #500, Minneapolis, MN 55402
612/339-7571

Vandades Continental
Carlos Obregon
6355 NW 36th St, Miami, FL 33166

Washington Review
Clarissa Wittenberg
Box 50132, Washington, DC 20004

WestArt
Martha Garcia
Box 6868, Auburn, CA 95604
916/885-0969

Where It's At
7204 Bucknell Dr, Austin, TX 78723
512/926-7954

Wildlife Art News
Robert Koehnke
PO Box 16246, St Louis Park, MN 55416

Window
Doug Hanson
PO Box 300128, Minneapolis, MN 55403

WNCN Art News
1180 Avenue of the Americas, New York, NY 10036

Womans Art Registry
2402 University Ave W, St Paul, MN 55114

The Works
Carolyn Brown
PO Box 131, Block Island, RI 02807

World Art
Ray Edgar
PO Box 480, Roseville, NSW, 2069 Australia

Specialty Magazines

Why a section in this source book entitled 'Specialty Magazines'? All businesses (artists included!) need to remember and be aware of the possibilities of publicity—and magazines are often where you get this publicity.

Send away for a 'review copy and rate card' on your business letterhead for magazines of interest to you. You will be able to see what the magazine has to offer you and your artwork (re: publicity possibilities). How do you fit into their editorial format? When you have the answer to this, call up the editor and give him a pitch for a story. For more information about the why and wherefore of publicity, see "Art Marketing Handbook" published by ArtNetwork, page 43 (916/432-7630).

A& D Business
Laura Fentress
800 Hudson St, Hoboken, NJ 07030

Alaska Airlines Magazine
Paul Temple
2701 First Ave #250, Seattle, WA 98121

American Desert
PO Box 1303, Desert Hot Springs, CA 92240

American Homestyle Magazine
110 5th Ave, New York, NY 10011

American Way Magazine
American Airlines Publications
PO Box 619640, DFW Airport, TX 76155

Architectural Digest
Paige Rense
6300 Wilshire Blvd 11Fl, Los Angeles, CA 90048
213/965-3700

Architectural Record
Carolyn DeWitt
1221 Ave of the Americas, New York, NY 10020

Architecture
Deborah Dietsch
1130 Connecticut Ave NW, Washington, DC 20036

Arts and Architecture
The Schindler House
835 N Kings Rd, Los Angeles, CA 90069

ASID Report
Joseph Pryweller
608 Massachusetts Ave NE, Washington, DC 07030

Azure
Nelda Rodgers
2 Silver Ave, Toronto, Ontario Canada M6R 3A2

Better Homes & Gardens
David Jordan
1716 Locust St, Des Moines, IA 50309

Business Interiors
PO Box 2060, Red Bank, NJ 07701

Caribbean Travel and Life
Veronica Staddart
8403 Colesville Rd #830, Silver Springs, MD 20910-3314

Changing Homes
1391 20th Ave, San Francisco, CA 94122

Computer Pictures Magazine
25 Bischoff Ave, Chappaqua, NY 10514

Condé Nast Traveler
Thomas Wallace
360 Madison Ave, New York, NY 10017

Contract
1515 Broadway, New York, NY 10036

Contract Design
Roger Yee
1515 Broadway, New York, NY 10036

Corporate Design
850 Third Ave, New York, NY 10022

Cruise & Vacation Views
60 E 42nd St #905, New York, NY 10165

Cruise Industry News
Oivind Mathisen
441 Lexington Ave #1209, New York, NY 10017

Decorating Ideas
707 Kautz Rd, St Charles, IL 60174

Catalogs & Magazines

Specialty Magazines (cont.)

Design Spirit
Suzanne Goodman
438 3rd St, Brooklyn, NY 11215

Design Times
Box 960, Cambridge, MA 02140

Design Today
Judith Cushman
PO Box 2754, High Point, NC 27261

Designers Illustrated
Julie Cam
4410 El Camino Real #111, Los Altos, CA
94022-1049

Designers Report
17 W 20th St, New York, NY 10011

Designers West
50 E 89th St, New York, NY 10028

Diversions
Marcus A Loy & Associates/Tom Passavant
14114 Dallas Pkwy #245, Dallas, TX 75240

Educated Traveler
Ann Waigand
PO Box 220822, Chantilly, VA 22022

Elle
1633 Broadway 42Fl, New York, NY 10019

Endless Vacation
Laurie Borman
3502 Woodview Ter, Indianapolis, IN
46268

Entertainair
Jack Horner
2549 Mosside Blvd #201, Monroeville,
PA 15146

Entrepreneur
PO Box 19787, Irvine, CA 92714

Entrepreneurial Woman
PO Box 19787, Irvine, CA 92714

Excursions
Richard Puracell
1018 E Indiana School Rd, Phoenix, AZ
85014

Family Circle
Jacqueline Leo
110 5th Ave, New York, NY 10011

Frequent Flyer
Henry Wall
1775 Broadway 19Fl, New York, NY 10019

Friendly Exchange
Paula Marshall
1912 Grand Ave, Des Moines, IA 50309

Good Housekeeping
John Carter
959 8th Ave, New York, NY 10019

Gracious Stays and Special Places
Helen Heath
2856 Hundred Oaks, Baton Rouge, LA
70806

Harper's Bazaar
1700 Broadway, New York, NY 10019

Haut Decor
Janet Verdeover
3290 NE 12th Ave, Oakland Park, FL 33334

Hawaiian Airlines Magazine
1188 Bishop St #2708, Honolulu, HI 96813

Hemispheres
Kate Greer
1301 Carolina St, Greensboro, NC 27401

Home Accents Today
200 S Main St, Highpoint, NC 27261

Home Business Journal
Marty Marsh
2536 E Impala Ave, Mesa, AZ 85204
602/892-6221

Horizon Air
Paul Frichtl
2701 First Ave #250, Seattle, WA 98121

House Beautiful
1700 Broadway, New York, NY 10019

IDEAS
PO Box 343392, Coral Gables, FL 33114

Interior Design Handbook
Columbia Communications
370 Lexington Ave, New York, NY 10017

Interiors
Jean Gorman
1515 Broadway, New York, NY 10036

Interiors & Sources
Katie Sosnowchik
450 Skokie Blvd #507, Northbrook, IL 60662

International Contract Magazine
Lisa Flochon
312 Dolomite Dr #217, Downsview, Ontario
Canada M3J 2N2

International Living
Kathleen Peddicord
824 E Baltimore St, Baltimore, MD 21202

International Travel News
David Tykol
2120 28th St, Sacramento, CA 95818

Islands
Joan Trapper
3886 State St, Santa Barbara, CA 93105

Ladies Home Journal
Myrna Blyth
100 Park Ave, New York, NY 10017

Latitudes South
Sharon Jaffe Dan
8403 Colesville Rd #830, Silver Springs, MD
20910

Leisure Air
Richard Teachout
8955 Washington Ave S, Minneapolis, MN
55439

McCall's
Kate White
110 5th Ave, New York, NY 10011

Metropolis
Susan Szenasy
177 E 87th St, New York, NY 10128

Metropolitan Home
1633 Broadway 42Fl, New York, NY 10019

Midwest Express Magazine
Eric Lucas
2701 First Ave #250, Seattle, WA 98121

Modern Maturity
Henry Fenwick
3200 E Carson St, Lakewood, CA 90712

Northwest Travel
Dave Peden
PO Box 18000, Florence, OR 97439

Progressive Architecture
Valerie Siaca
600 Summer St, Stamford, CT 06904

Recommend
Susan Mann
5879 NW 15th St #120, Miami Lakes, FL
33014

Redbook
Ellen Levine
224 W 57th St, New York, NY 10019

Relax
Mary Kaye Stray
2 Illinois Ct 24 Fl, Chicago, IL 60601

Resorts & Great Hotels
123 W Padre, Santa Barbara, CA 93105
702/435-4569

Residential Interiors
1515 Broadway, New York, NY 10036

Santa Barbara Magazine
Marsha Ban
216 E Victoria St, Santa Barbara, CA 93101

SE Travel Professional
1200 NW 78th Ave #201, Miami, FL 33126

Seafood Leader
Martha Brouwer
1115 NW 46th St, Seattle, WA 98107
Have an annual call for fine artists who create sea-related artwork.

Senior Travel Tips
Elana Andersen
5281 Scotts Valley Dr, Scotts Valley, CA
95066

Catalogs & Magazines

Specialty Magazines (cont.)

Sky Magazine
Lidia de Leon
600 Corporate Dr #300, Ft Lauderdale, FL
33334

Sky Magazine
Atlanta International Airport, Atlanta, GA
30320

Sojourns
Barry Parker
PO Box 1385, Brentwood, TN 37024

Sunset
William Marken
80 Willow Rd, Menlo Park, CA 94025

Tour & Travel News
Jeff Barrington
600 Community Dr, Manhasset, NY 10030

Travel a la Carte
Donna Carter
136 Walton St, Port Hope, Ontario Canada
L1A 1N5

Travel & Leisure
Nancy Novogrod
1120 Ave of the Americas, New York, NY
10036

Travel & Tourism
Marj Jensen
PO Box 43563, Washington, DC 20010

Travel Gent Magazine
Erick Friedheim
801 2nd Ave 12Fl, New York, NY 10017

Travel Holiday
28 W 23rd St, New York, NY 10010

Travel Management Newsletter
Martha Deutsch
1775 Broadway 19Fl, New York, NY 10019

Travel News
Matthew Wiseman
111 2nd Ave NE 15Fl, St Petersburg, FL
33701

Travel Smart
JH Teison
40 Beachdale Rd, Dobbs Ferry, NY 10522

Travel Trade News Edition
Joel Abele
15 W 44th St, New York, NY 10036

Travel Trends
Peter Mason
750 3rd Ave 12Fl, New York, NY 10017

Travel World News
Sara Southworth
1 Morgan Ave, Norwalk, CT 06851

Travelage East
Ed Sullivan
1775 Broadway, New York, NY 10019

Travelin Magazine
Gary Turner
PO Box 23005, Eugene, OR 97402

Travelore Report
Ted Barkus
1512 Spruce St, Philadelphia, PA 19102

Traveltips
PO Box 188, Flushing , NY 11358

TWA Ambassador
Joseph Mangise
100 S Bedford Rd, Mt Kisco, NY 10549

US Air Magazine
Terri Barnes
1301 Carolina St #200, Greensboro, NC
27401

Vacations
1502 Augusta Dr #415, Houston, TX 77057

VISTA USA
30400 Van Dyke Ave, Warren, MI 48093

Vitality Magazine
Barbara Floria
8080 N Central Expressway #1510, Dallas, TX
75206

Voyager International
PO Box 2777, Westport, CT 06880

Where New York
Michael Tucker
600 3rd Ave 15Fl, New York, NY 10016

Regional Directories

These regional directories will help you locate fine art shows, galleries, consultants, grants and other art-related information in specific areas throughout the country. "Art Marketing Sourcebook, Second Edition" has a section entitled 'Show Directories' which also lists regional directories.

Access: A Guide to the Visual Arts in Washington State
Allied Arts of Seattle
107 S Main, Seattle, WA 98104
Lists alternative, non-profit, commercial and university and museum spaces.

ACF News
PO Box 371, Glenshaw, PA 15116
412/487-7715
Bi-monthly publication covering arts and crafts festivals in the eastern U.S./800 listings each issue/$15 annual subscription.

Art and Craft Fairs—Wisconsin
Wisconsin Arts Board
101 Wilson St, Madison, WI 53702
Free.

Artist's Guide for Chicago and the Illinois Region
Chicago Artists' Coalition
5 W Grand Ave, Chicago, IL 60610
312/670-2060
Lists 253 commercial, alternative, co-op, university and museum spaces.

Artists' Guide to Philadelphia
PO Box 8755, Philadelphia, PA 19101

Arts Directory
Arts Council of Hillsborough County
1000 N Ashley Dr #316, Tampa, FL 33602
Over 200 art groups in Hillsborough County/$8ppd.

The Arts Resource and Information Center
The Minneapolis Institute of Arts
2400 3rd Ave S, Minneapolis, MN 55405
612/870-3131

Directory of Visual Art Organizations in NJ
PO Box 2195, Westfield, NJ 07091
$3.50.

Exhibits, Fairs, Festivals and Performances
Tennessee Arts Commission/Stephanie Tallman
404 James Robertson Pkwy #160, Nashville, TN 37243
615/741-1701
Free.

Fairs and Festivals
Arts Education Services
604 Goodell Bldg, Box 33260, U of MA, Amherst, MA 01003
413/545-2360
$15.50ppd.

Festival Hoppers
Creative Chaos Press
Have a set of four guides for various parts of the country.

Festival Network
PO Box 18839, Asheville, NC 28814
800/200-3737
Lists over 900 festivals and events/one year subscription $35.

Festivals
Art America
PO Box 550, Moorehead City, NC 28557
Published quarterly.

Gallery Spaces for Vermont Artists
VMGA
PO Box 10, Shelburne, VT 05482
802/985-3345
66 galleries and high-end craft venues/$10ppd.

Grants and Residencies
Dutchess County Art Association
55 N Noxon St, Poughkeepsie, NY 12601
914/471-2250
$6/10-15 pages.

Guide to Grants for Minnesota Artists
Minnesota State Arts Board
432 Summit Ave, St Paul, MN 55102
612/297-2603
Free.

Guide to New England's Art Facilities: Volume II, Museums and Galleries
New England Foundation for the Arts
617/492-2914

Catalogs & Magazines

Regional Directories (cont.)

Illinois Art Fair Directory
Illinois Arts Council
100 W Randolph #10-500, Chicago, IL 60601
312/814-6750

Iowa Calendar of Events
Dept of Economic Development
200 E Grand Ave, Des Moines, IA 50309
515/242-4705

Maine Cultural Guide
Maine Crafts Association
PO Box 228, Deer Isle, ME 04627
207/348-9943

Michigan Arts Fair Directory
MCAC
1200 Sixth St #1180, Detroit, MI 48226-2461
313/256-3731
Free with #10 SASE (78¢).

Minnesota Arts Directory
Box 580320, Minneapolis, MN 55458-0320
612/871-0813
Annual source book of shows, artists, businesses, services and organizations.

New York Contemporary Art Galleries
Renee Phillips Associates
200 E 72 St #26-L, New York, NY 10021
$19.95 ppd.

Ohio Arts Festivals and Competitions Directory
Ohio Arts Council
727 E Main St, Columbus, OH 43205-1796
$1.19 in stamps.

Oklahoma Arts and Crafts Review
Sheila Gray
601 W Lynn Dr, El Reno, OK 73036-1422
405/262-8666

On Exhibit: A Guide to Galleries & Exhibition Spaces in Sarasota
Art Publicity
PO Box 49493, Sarasota, Fl 34236
Send 52¢ SASE.

Portland Art Gallery Guide
Art Media
902 S Yamhill, Portland, OR 97205
503/239-7279

Public Hangings
The City Gallery
NY City Dept of Cultural Affairs
2 Columbus Cir, New York, NY 10019
Lists more than 80 alternative spaces in NYC.

Ronay Guide
A Step Ahead Ltd
2950 Pangborn Rd, Decatur, GA 30033-1822
404/939-2452
Covers GA, FL, AL, TN, NC, SC, VA.

Southern Oregon Media Directory
33 N Central Ave #308, Medford, OR 97501
503/779-2820

Thy Neighbor's Talent
McClintocks MX-Ranch
HCR 1 Box 75, Baldwin, ND 58521
Send SASE.

Vermont Directory of Foundations
CPG Enterprises
Box 199, Shaftsbury, VT 05262
802/447-0256

The Virginia Guide to Arts & Crafts Shows
Forever Country
PO Box 990, New Market, VA 22844
703/740-8057
Lists over 500 shows and festivals/$9.95 ppd.

Virginia Visual Artists' Resource Directory
Parks/Balfour
PO Box 4831, Richmond, VA 23220
804/353-2610 804/233-2238

Washington Art: A Guide to Galleries, Art Consultants and Museums
Art Calendar
PO Box 199, Upper Fairmount, MD 21867
703/651-9150
Lists 135 commercial galleries, 58 art centers, 23 consultants and 23 museums/$13.95.

Where the Shows Are
PO Box 453, Edgewater, Fl 32132-0453
904/428-0173
$17ppd single issue/$32 four issues.

Wisconsin Art & Craft Directory
Wisconsin Arts Board
101 Wilson St 1Fl, Madison, WI 53702
608/266-0190
Send 9x12 with $1.93 SASE.

Reference Directories

Make the library a place you spend some time doing research. Begin your research with the assistance of your librarian. You can photocopy pages from reference manuals that will eventually be used to compile your mailing lists. Following are some reference books you might use. Libraries subscribe to different journals, so ask your librarian for a replacement-type reference book if they don't have these particular ones.

American Institute of Architects
1911 First Ave, Seattle, WA 98101
206/448-4938

Art Business News Annual Directory
800/346-0085

Art in America Annual Buyers Guide
212/941-2800
Many references by style and subject matter.

Bacons Directories
332 S Michigan Ave 9FL, Chicago, IL 60604
Publicity Checker
International Publicity Checker
Media Alert
Radio and TV Directory

Directory of Greeting Card Sales Representatives
Greeting Card Association
1200 G St NW #760, Washington, DC 20005
202/393-1778

Directory of US Greeting Card Sales Reps
Terriere Marketing
6323 SW 60th Ave, Portland, OR 97221
503/245-5703
Over 400 individuals in 50 states/$100.

EBSCO
5724 Highway 280 E, Birmingham, AL 35242
800/826-3024
Periodical Directory

Gale Research Inc
Book Tower, Detroit, MI 48226
Encyclopedia of Associations
Directory of Publications and Broadcast Media
Trade Show Directory

Gebbies All-in-One Directory
Box 1000, New Paltz, NY 12561
914/255-7560
Afro-American Publications
Hispanic Publications

National Directory of Arts and Education Support by Business Corporations
Washington International Arts Letter
PO Box 9005, Washington, DC 20003

National Directory of Giftware and Stationery Reps
Rep Network/Office Works Corporation
913 W Van Buren, #6B, Chicago, IL 60607
312/733-7255
Divided into various regions/$79.98.

National Directory of Magazines

National Trade and Professional Asssociations of America
Columbia Books Inc
1212 New York Ave NW #330, Washington, DC 20005
202/898-0662

Oxbridge Communications
150 5th Ave, New York, NY 10011
800/955-0231
Standard Periodical Directory

Reed Reference Publishing
121 Chanlon Rd, PO Box 31, New Providence, NJ 07974
800/521-8110
Ulrichs International Periodical Directory
Literary Market Place
Trade Show Directory

Standard Rate & Data Services

Thomas Publishing Co
1 Penn Plz, New York, NY 10001
Register of Manufacturers

Todd Publications
PO Box 301, West Nyack, NY 10994
800/747-1056
Guide to free product publicity.

Catalogs & Magazines

Reference Directories
(cont.)

TV News Contacts
Television Contacts
Radio Contacts
Cable Contacts
News Bureau Contacts

UK Wealth Directory/USA Wealth Directory
Rowland Lybrand of London
28 Wheatley Ct, Mixenden, Halifax,
W Yorkshire HX2 8Ql England

Direct Marketing

Association of 3rd Class Mail Users
1725 K St NW, Washington DC 20006

Direct Marketing Association/DMA
230 Park Ave, New York, NY 10017

Mailing Lists

*Many major libraries have these reference direc-
tories to locate mailing lists:*
Standard Rate and Data Direct Mail List
Direct Mail Marketing Place
Who's Who in Direct Marketing
Literary Market Place

American Business Directories
5711 S 86th Cir, PO Box 27347, Omaha, NE
68127-4146
402/593-4600

ArtNetwork
PO Box 1268, 18757 Wildflower Dr,
Penn Valley, CA 95946
916/432-7630
*A variety of small and large lists for artists and
artworld professionals' promotion.*

ParaLists
Dan Poynter
PO Box 4232, Santa Barbara, CA 93140
800/PARAPUB 805/968-7277
*Put together by a book publisher for promotion
of their books, ie. aviation magazines, automo-
bile magazines, horse magazines, etc.*

Twin Peaks Press
PO Box 129, Vancouver, WA 98666-0129
800/637-2256 206/694-2462
*Co-op mailings and mailing lists; many genres of
groups.*

Wilson Marketing Group
11924 W Washington Blvd, Los Angeles, CA
90066
800/445-2089
*Gift shops at hospitals and many other specific
lists.*

CHAPTER V

●●●●●●●●●●●●●●●●●●●●●●

PUBLICATIONS

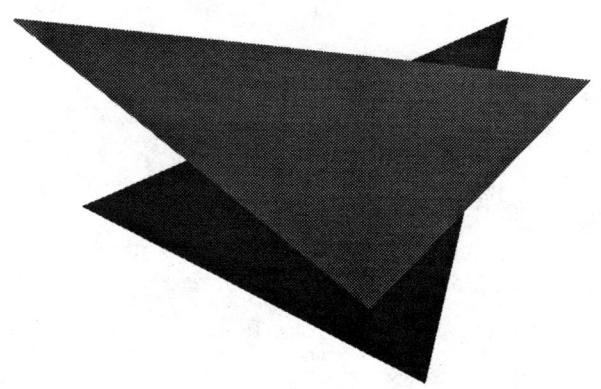

To keep on top of your business you must constantly be researching the marketplace and discovering new ideas. These books will help you do just that. Many of these books can be checked out from your local library, or if need be, your inter-library loan service. In some cases we have listed the address where you can order the book. Some of the larger publishers are noted with an * after their name. Their address is listed on pages 74-77. Book titles that have ** preceding their title are books sold by ArtNetwork (916/432-7630).

Business

110 Ideas for Organizing Your Business by Paulette Ensign
Organizing Solutions
PO Box AC, Katonah, NY 10536
A brochure/$3.55.

Advertising Management by David Aacker and John Myers
Prentice Hall

The Art Biz: The Covert World of Collectors, Dealers, Auction Houses, Museums and Critics by Alice Goldfarb Marquis
Contemporary Books*

**Art Charts by Sue Viders
Charts to help organize your career. Full of marketing ideas.

The Artist in Business: Basic Business Practices by Craig Creeszen
Arts Extension Service*

The Artist in the Marketplace by Patricia Fischer

The Artist's Guide to His Market by Betty Chamberlain
Watson-Guptill*

Artist's Pocket Guidebook
Chroma Acrylics
105 Bucky Dr, Lititz, PA 17543
Free 48-page brochure on procedures, techniques, tips and guidelines.

Auction Index Inc
30 Valentine Park, Newton, MA 02165

Business Etiquette by Jacqueline Dunckel

The Business of Art by Diane Cochrane
Watson-Guptill*

**The Business of Art by Lee Evan Caplin

The Business of Being an Artist by Daniel Grant
Allworth Press*

Developing the Press Packet
Media Distribution Co-op
1745 Louisiana St, Lawrence, KS 66044

Do-It-Yourself Marketing Research by George Edward Breen
McGraw-Hill*

Do-It-Yourself Publicity by David Ramacitti

The Entrepreneurial Woman by Sandra Winston
Newsweek Books

**Fine Art Publicity by Susan Abbott

The Fine Artist's Guide to Showing and Selling Your Work
Northlight*

Getting Your Act Together: Goal Setting for Fun, Health and Profit by George Morrisey
John Wiley & Sons

Good Show! A Practical Guide for Temporary Exhibitions by Lothar Witteborg

**Guerrilla Marketing in the 90s by Jay Conrad Levinson

Guerrilla PR by Michael Levine

Homemade Money by Barbara Brabec
BPC
PO Box 2137, Naperville, IL 60566
$14.95.

How to Advertise: A Handbook for Small Business by Sandra Linville Dean
Enterprise Publishing

How to Get Results with Publicity
700 Black Horse Pike #110, Blackwood, NJ 08012

Publications

How to Make Your Advertising Twice as Effective at Half the Cost by Herschell Gordon Lewis
  Graphic Artists Book Club*

How to Organize a Small Business by Clifford M Baumback, Kenneth Lawyer and Pearce C Kelley
  Prentice-Hall

How to Read a Financial Report by John A Tracey

How to Start Your Own Business. . . and Succeed by Arthur H Kuriloff and John M Hemphill
  McGraw-Hill*

How to Win the Battle Against Inflation with a Small Business by Murray Miller and Franz Serdaheyly
  Enterprise Publishing

Living By Your Brush Alone by Edna Wagner Piersol

Mayer International Art Auction Records
  Distributed Art Publishers*

Open Studio Event: An Artist's Planning Guide
  Artists Foundation Inc*

The Organization Map by Pam McClellan
  F&W Publications*

The Paper Pile-Up by Stephanie Culp
  Writers Digest Books*

Penny-Pinching Pointers for Everyone by Edmund J Gross
  Halls of Ivy Press

Personal Selling Power
  PO Box 5467, Fredericksburg, VA 22403
  800/752-7355

Pocket Media Guide
  307 W 36th St, New York, NY 10018
  Lists national media sources. Free if requested on business letterhead.

Popcorn Report: Your Company, Your World, Your Life by Faith Popcorn

Small Business Development Catalog
  Entrepreneur Magazine Group*

**Small Time Operator - How to Start Your Own Business, Keep Your Books, Pay Your Taxes, and Stay Out of Trouble by Bernard Kamoroff, CPA

The Successful Promoter by Ted Schwarz
  Contemporary Books*

Taming the Marketing Jungle by Silvana Clark
  Memory Makers
  3024 Haggin St, Bellingham, WA 98226

Tools for Business Success
  PSI Research*

Your Business Plan by Dennis J Sargent
  Oregon Small Business Network
  44 W Broadway #501, Eugene, OR 97401
  503/726-2250
  $25ppd.

Design

The Best of Brochure Design
  Rockport Publishers*

The Best of Business Card Design
  Rockport Publishers*

Business Card Graphics
  Northlight*

Business Card Graphics 2
  Books Nippan*

Business Cards: Dynamic Graphic Design
  Rizzoli*

The Colorist Newsletter Digest
  4 Fourth Pl, Garden City, NY 11530
  $20 quarterly.

Create the Perfect Sales Piece: A do-it-yourself guide to producing brochures, catalogs, etc.

Creating Brochures & Booklets by Val Adkins
  Northlight*

Designer's Commonsense Business Book by Barbara Ganim

Publications

Fresh Ideas in Letterhead and Business Card Design by Diana Martin & Mary Cooper
Northlight*

Fundamentals of Copy and Layout by Dennis C Schick and Albert C Book
NTC Publishing Group*

Getting It Printed by Mark Beach
Northlight*

Great Type and Lettering Design
Northlight*

How to Design Trademarks and Logos by John Murphy & Michael Rowe

In Color
US Press
PO Box 640, Valdosta, GA 31603-0640
A magazine explaining color printing.

International Logo Types
Graphic Artists Book Club*

Letterhead & Logo Designs 2
Graphic Artists Book Club*

Letterheads: One Hundred Years of Great Design
Chronicle Books

One Minute Designer by Roger C Parker

Print's Best Business Card Graphics
Graphic Artists Book Club*

Print's Best Letterheads & Business Cards 2
Northlight*

Producing Flyers, Folders and Brochures

A Typeface Sourcebook
Rockport Publishers*

Exhibition Catalogs

Blazer Art Books*
Send for free catalog of hundreds of hard-to-find art publications.

Gallery
Drawer 9, Brewster, NY 10509
Over 8000 new and out-of-print books and exhibition catalogs exclusively on American art and artists.

Funding/Grants
(See section on Grants & Residencies)

General

American Art Directory
RR Bowker*
Lists over 7000 museums, art libraries, art organizations/$159.95.

Art For Work by Marjory Jacobson
Harvard Business School Press
The new renaissance for corporate collecting.

The Art of Selling Art

The Art of Showing Art by James K Reeves
Council Oak Books
800/247-8850

Artisthelp: The Artist's Guide to Human and Social Services edited by Joan Jeffri
Neal-Schuman
23 Leonard St, New York, NY 10013
35 pages of social and health services for artists.

Artist's Guide to Getting & Having a Successful Exhibition by Robert S Perskey
Consultants Press*

Artists of the Page: Interviews with Children's Book Illustrators by Sylvia & Kenneth Marantz

Ayer's Directory of Publications

The Care and Handling of Art Objects: Practices in the Metropolitan Museum of Art by Marjorie Shelley
Harry N Abrams

The Care of Photography by Siegfried Rempel
Lyons & Burford*

The Care of Prints and Drawings by Margaret Holben Ellis
AASLH Press
172 2nd Ave #303, Nashville, TN 37201

Caring For Your Art: A Guide for Artists, Collectors, Galleries, and Art Institutions by Jill Snyder
Allworth Press*

Publications

Caring for Your Collections by Joyce Hill Stoner
Harry N Abrams

Celebrity Directory
Axiom Information Resources
PO Box 8015, Ann Arbor, MI 48107
Lists over 8,000 celebrities: film and TV stars, athletes, recording artists, politicians and authors/$42.95.

Chase's Annual Events
Contemporary Books*
Over 10,000 entries. Get ideas for possible shows from here.

Corporate 1000
Monitor Publishing Co
104 5th Ave 2Fl, New York, NY 10011
Lists the thousand largest companies in the U.S/ $135 per year for four quarterly issues.

Creating Space: A Real Estate Development Guide for Artists by Cheryl Kartes
American Council for the Arts*

Directory of Artists' Slide Registries by Suzy Ticho

Directory of Sources for International Traveling Exhibitions
International Council of Museums
Washington, DC
Lists international organizations that manage traveling exhibitions, including contact information.

Dodge Reports
FW Dodge Division, McGraw-Hill Information Systems
1221 Ave of the Americas, New York, NY 10020
212/512-3711
Daily computerized printouts of construction projects. Good for artists looking for commissions, especially sculptors or producers of large objects. Service is sold in minimum three-month units and is based on geographical areas, the larger the area covered the more expensive the service. Current minimum is $34 per month per city. Purchasers can select the type of construction they are interested in - theaters, religious buildings, public buildings, etc. Most architects and engineering firms get Dodge Reports. You may be able to get one of their old copies.

Encyclopedia of Associations

Going Public
Arts Extension Services*
Information on 200 ongoing art programs across the U.S. in the public and private sector: how to contact, artists' eligibility, etc./$23.45ppd.

Guide to American Art Schools by John D Werenko
Penguin Books

Guide to Eliminating Clutter
Learning Annex
291 Geary #510, San Francisco, CA 94102
415/788-5500

Guide to Maintenance of Outdoor Sculpture
American Institute of Conservation
1717 K St NW #301, Washington, DC 20006
202/452-9545
$15ppd.

A Handbook on the Care of Paintings by Caroline K Kech

Health Insurance for the Self-Employed by Lenore Janecek
Allworth Press*

How to Enter & Win Contests by Alan Gadney

How to Photograph Paintings by Nat Bukar

How to Photograph Works of Art by Sheldon Collins

Individual's Guide to Organizing a Traveling Art Exhibition by Raymond Markarian

Insight - On Sites by Stacey Paleologos-Harris
Explores the issues of art in public places. Insight on the process of selecting artists and art for public places.

New York State Contract Reporter
New York State Dept of Economic Development Division for Small Business
A weekly newsletter announcing contracting opportunities of $5,000 or more within NY.

Off the Wall: Robert Rauschenberg and the Art World of Our Time by Calvin Tomkins
Penguin Books

Office Clutter Cure by Don Aslett
Northlight*

Official Museum Directory
RR Bowker*
Lists aquariums, botanical gardens, planetariums, zoos, nature centers, historic homes, art associations.

Our Government and the Arts by Livingston Biddle
Biddle was the previous director of the NEA. He takes us through the history of its development.

Permanence and Care of Color Photographs: Traditional and Digital Color Prints, Color Negatives, Slides and Motion Pictures by Henry Wilhelm
Preservation Publishing Co
PO Box 567, Grinnell, IA 50112
515/236-0900

**Photographing Your Artwork by Russell Hart

Publicity Manual by Kate Kelly

The Right Frame by Henry Heydenryk Jr
Lyons and Burford*

Safe Practices in the Arts and Crafts: A Studio Guide by Gail Coningsby Barazani
College Art Association*

Talking With Artists by Pat Cummings
Bradbury Press

Traveler's Guide to Museum Exhibitions
Museum Guide Publications
PO Box 25369, 1619 31 St NW,
Washington, DC 20007
202/338-1500
$19ppd.

Ulrich's Periodicals Directory
RR Bowker*
Over 3,681 markets.

US Publicity Directory

Way To Go by Stephen Horne
Gallery Association of New York State
Box 345, Hamilton, NY 13346-0345
315/824-2510
Shows how to ship your artwork/$10.

Greeting Cards

The Complete Guide to Greeting Card Design & Illustration by Eva Szela
Northlight*

Designer Greetings by Patrick Mitchell

Gift and Stationery Business
Gralla Publications
1515 Broadway, New York, NY 10036
212/869-1300

Greeting Card Design by Joanne Fink

Greeting Cards by Takenobu Igarashi

Greetings Magazine
307 5th Ave 16 Fl, New York, NY 10016
212/679-6677

How to Write and Sell Greeting Cards, Bumper Stickers, T-Shirts and Other Fun Stuff by Molly Wigand
Writers Digest Books*

Starting Your Own Greeting Card Company: How to Survive and Prosper by Sandy Glain
PO Box 15, Balboa Island, CA 92662
$18ppd.

Working with Wholesale Giftware Reps by Jill Ford
Rep Registry
Box 2306, Capistrano Beach, CA 92624
714/240-3333

Health Hazards

Art Hazard News
Center for Safety in the Arts
5 Beekman St #1030, New York, NY 10038
212/227-6220
They have a variety of other publications covering safety in the arts/$21.00 per year.

Artist Beware, Second Edition by Michael M Cann
Lyons & Burford*

Artists Complete Health and Safety Guide by Monona Rossol
Allworth Press*

Health Hazards in Photography by Susan Shaw and Monona Rossol

Publications

Making Art Safely by Merle Spandorfer, Deborah Curtis & Jack Snyder
Van Nostrand Reinhold*

Jobs

Art Career Guide by Donald Holden
Watson Guptill*

Art Works
Resources & Counseling for the Arts
612/292-4381
A free guide for would-be arts administrators that covers almost every issue that job seekers need to consider.

Career Resources List for Visual Artists
Union of Independent Colleges of Art

Careers in the Visual Arts by Dee Ito
Watson Guptill*

Guide to American Art Schools edited by John D Wreneko
Penguin Books

Jobs in Arts and Media Management by Stephen Langley and James Abruzzo
American Council for the Arts*

Jobs in the Arts & Arts Administration

MFA Programs in the Visual Arts: A Directory
College Art Association*

National Resource Guide for Placement of Artists edited by Cheryl Slean and Warren Christensen
NNAP*

Opportunities in the Visual Arts by Mark Salmon

The Robert Half Way by Robert Half

Where to Start Career Planning
Cornell U Career Center

Legal

(See section on Business, Lawyers & Accountants)

Non-Profit Info

ARIS Funding Reports
Academic Research Information Systems
415/558-8133
Grant alert newsletter/$115 per year.

Directory of Minority Art Organizations
NEA

Fundraising for Non-Profit Groups by Joyce Young

Guide to Women's Art Organizations by Cynthia Navaretta

How to Form a Non-Profit Corporation by Anthony Mancuso
Nolo Press*

Non-Profit Partners
Heights International Publishing
4502 Groveland Rd, PO Box 18937,
University Heights, OH 44118
They have an entire catalog of books regarding non-profit organizations.

To Be or Not To Be: An Artist's Guide to Not-for-Profit Corporations
Volunteer Lawyers for the Arts
1 E 53rd St 6Fl, New York, NY 10022
212/319-2787
A 12-page booklet to help you investigate forming a legal entity through which you can conduct your artistic activities.

Printmaking

Benefits and Profits from Art Prints
Art Print Publishers
PO Box 9100, Seattle, WA 98109
$9.95ppd.

The Complete Printmaker by Clare Romano and John Ross

Getting It Printed by Beach, Shapiro, Russon

A Guide to the Collection and Care of Original Prints by Carl Zigrosser

How to Silkscreen on Cylindrical and Contoured Surfaces by Thomas Gilson

Printing News Magazine
516/845-2700

**Printmaking: A Beginning Handbook
By William C Maxwell**

**Printmaking Without a Press by Erickson and Sproul
Prints and the Print Market by TD Donson**

Silk Screen Techniques for the Artist by Kenneth Auvil

Textile Screen Printing by Albert Kosloff

US ART Guide to Print Values
USArt Magazine
220 S 6th St #500, Minneapolis, MN 55402
612/339-7571

Publishing

Art Print Index
1233 Quarry Ln #125, Pleasanton, CA 94566
800/346-5924

Directory of Book, Catalog, and Magazine Printers by John Kremer
Lists overseas printers for inexpensive and beautiful color printing.

Preparing Art for Printing by Bernard Stone and Arthur Echstin

Print Workshops by Carol Pulin
711 E St NE, Washington, DC 20002
A booklet listing print workshops in US and Canada/$10.

**** Producing and Marketing Prints by Sue Viders**

Religious

Christian Symbols, Ancient and Modern by Heather Child and Dorothy Colles

Contemporary Synagogue Art by Avram Kampf

Crafts of Israel by Ruth Dayan

Ecclesiastical Crafts by Bucky King

Embroideries and Fabrics for the Synagogue and Home by Lillian Freehof and Bucky King

How to Create Your Own Design by Bill Hinz and Jim Hinz

The Jewish Catalog: A Do-It-Yourself Kit by Michael Strassfeld

Textile Art in the Church by Marion Ireland

The Western Synagogue Through Two Centuries by Arthur Barnett

Residencies

(See section on Grants & Residencies)

Taxes

The Art of Deduction: Income Taxation for Performing, Visual, and Literary Artists by Kim Marios

Future Safe, The Present is the Future
Artist Trust
1402 Third Ave, Seattle, WA 98101
Send a 9x12 SASE with 78¢ postage for this free brochure on estate planning.

How To Pay Less Tax
Consumer Guide Publishing

Julian Block's Year-Round Tax Strategies
3 Washington Sq, Larchmont, NY 10538

Starting and Succeeding in Your Own Business

A Tax Guide for Artists and Arts Organizations edited by Herrick Lidstone

The Tax Reliever: A Guide for the Artist by Richard Helleloid

Taxes and the Individual Artist by Jeffrey Abouaf

What Everyone Wants to Know About Law
US News & World Report Management Library

Your Income Tax by JK Lasser
Simon & Schuster
1230 Avenue of the Americas, New York, NY 10020
Updated annually. Can be found at all major bookstores.

Publications

Art Business Book Publishers

Write or call for free brochures for these business and art book publishers and distributors.

Allworth Press
10 E 23rd St #400, New York, NY 10010
212/777-8395

American Council for the Arts
1 E 53rd St, New York, NY 10022
800/321-4510 212/223-2787

Art Book Services
PO Box 360, Hughsonville, NY 12537
800/247-9955

Art Resources International
5813 Nevada Ave NW, Washington, DC 20015-2547
202/363-6806

Artesia Press
PO Box 21, Springfield, OR 97477
503/746-0094

Artist Resource Service
PO Box 181, Harvard, MA 01451-0181

Artists Foundation Inc
860 Harrison Ave #309, Boston, MA 03127
617/859-3810

ArtNetwork
PO Box 1268, 18757 Wildflower Dr, Penn Valley, CA 95946
916/432-7630

Arts Action Issues
PO Box 401082, Brooklyn, NY 11240-1082

Arts Extension Services
Continuing Ed/U of MA at Amherst
Goodell Bldg, Amherst, MA 01003
413/545-2360

Bargain Books
Edward R Hamilton
PO Box 358, Falls Village, CT 06031

Barnes & Noble Catalog
26 Fifth Ave, New York, NY 10011
212/807-0099

Blazer Art Books
Box 693, Vineyard Haven, MA 02568

Book Exchange
90 W Market St, Corning, NY 14830
607/936-4732

Books Nippan
800/562-1410

California Lawyers for the Arts
Fort Mason Center, Bldg C #255, San Francisco, CA 94123
415/775-7200

Center for Arts Information
1285 Ave of the Americas 3Fl, New York, NY 10019
212/787-6557 ext. 122

Chester Book Co
4 Maple St, Chester, CT 06412
203/526-9887

College Art Association/CAA
275 7th Ave, New York, NY 10001
212/691-1051

Consultant Press
163 Amsterdam, New York, NY 10023
212/838-8640

Contemporary Books
180 N Stetson Ave, Chicago, IL 60601
312/540-4500

Council for Business and the Arts in Canada
PO Box 7 #1507, Simpson Tower, 401 Bay St, Toronto, Ontario Canada M5H 2Y4
416/869-3016

Daedalus Books
4601 Decatur St, Hyattsville, MO 20781
800/333-5489

DATA Inc
70 Audubon St, New Haven, CT 06510
203/772-1345

Decor
330 N 4th St, St Louis, MO 63102
314/421-5445

Discount Books
3701 N Mill Rd, Vineland, NJ 08360

Distributed Art Publishers
636 Broadway 12Fl, New York, NY 10012
800/338-BOOK

Dover Publications
31 E 2nd St, Mineola, NY 11501
516/294-7000
Various books on art history, theory and instruction.

Entrepreneur Magazine Group
PO Box 50370, Boulder, CO 80321
800/421-2300

F&W Publications
800/289-0963

The Foundation Center
79 Fifth Ave, New York, NY 10003
800/424-9836 212/620-4230

Gould Trading
7 E 17 St, New York, NY 10003
212/243-2306
Photography books.

Guerrilla Marketing
800/748-6444
All kinds of books on innovative marketing and PR.

Hacker Art Books
45 W 57th St, New York, NY 10019
212/688-7600

HarperCollins
10 E 53 St, New York, NY 10022
800/237-5534

Image Press
Peter Gould
89 5th Ave #903, New York, NY 10003
212/675-3707

Lark Books
50 College St, Asheville, NC 28801
800/284-3388

Lyons & Burford
31 W 21 St, New York, NY 10010
212/620-9580

McGraw Hill
800/722-4726

Mix Bookshelf
6400 Hollis #12, Emeryville, CA 94608
510/653-3307

National Association of Desktop Publishers/ NADTP
PO Box 1020, Sewickly, PA 15143
800/435-7116 412/741-0609

NAEA
1916 Association Dr, Reston, VA 22091
703/860-8000

National Center for Nonprofit Boards
2000 L St NW #510W, Washington, DC 20036-4907
202/452-6262
Books on the nonprofit sector.

NNAP
935 W Ave 37, Los Angeles, CA 90065
213/222-4035

Nolo Press
950 Parker St, Berkeley, CA 94710
800/992-6656 510/704-2248
Legal books.

Northlight
800/289-0963

NTC Publishing Group
4255 W Touhy Ave, Lincolnwood, IL 60646
708/679-5500
General business books.

Photo-Eye Books
376 Garcia St, Santa Fe, NM 87501
505/988-4955

PPFA
4305 Sarellen Rd, Richmond, VA 23231
804/226-0430

Print Books
3200 Tower Oaks Blvd, Rockville, MD 20852

Printed Matter
77 Wooster St, New York, NY 10012
212/925-0325

Publications

Art Business Book Publishers (cont.)

Promotional Perspectives
1829 W Stadium Blvd #101, Ann Arbor, MI
48103-4501
313/994-0007
Small catalog of books and newsletters.

PSI Research
300 N Valley Dr, Grants Pass, OR 97526
800/228-2275 503/479-9464

Pyramid Books
214 Derby St, Salem, MA 01970
508/745-7171

Reed Reference Publishers
800/521-8110

Reference Book Center
175 Fifth Ave, New York, NY 10010
212/677-2160

Rizzoli
300 Park Ave S, New York, NY 10010
800/522-6657

Rockport Publishers
800/289-0963

RR Bowker
800/521-8110

Self-Counsel Press
1704 N State St, Bellingham, WA 98225
800/663-3007 206/676-4530
All kinds of business books.

US Government
Superintendent of Documents
PO Box 371954, Pittsburgh, PA 15250
Write for free business catalog.

Van Nostrand Reinhold
115 Fifth Ave, New York, NY 10003
212/254-3232

Vesper Publishing
PO Box 150, Kenvil, NJ 07847
201/927-9185

Watson-Guptill
800/ART-TIPS

Whole Earth Review
27 Gate Five Road, Sausalito, CA 94965
415/332-1716

Whole Work Catalog
PO Box 339, Boulder, CO 80306
303-447-1087

Writers Digest Books
800/289-0963

Book Clubs

Doubleday Art Book Club
317/541-8920

Graphic Artists Book Club
PO Box 12526, Cincinnati, OH 45212
513/531-8250

Northlight Book Club
1507 Dana St, Cincinnati, OH 45207
800/289-0963

Print Book Club
3200 Tower Oaks Blvd, Rockville, MD
20852-9787

Wildlife Art News Book Club
800/626-0934

Foreign Publications

Across Europe—The Artist's Personal Guide to Opportunity and Action
AN Publications
Box 23, Sunderland, England
Resources in over 20 countries.

ARLIS Union List of Periodicals on Art Design and Related Subjects edited by John Kirby
Art Libraries Society/Susan St Clair
Kingston Polytechnic, Knights Park
Kingston-upon-Thames, England KT12QJ
Contains entries for over 5,000 art periodicals with locations and details in the UK.

The Artists Directory (British)

The Artists Guide (British)

International Directory of Arts
Gale Publishing
Covers over 137 countries/$148.

Who's Who in Art
Gale Publishing
Mostly British artists/$90.

CHAPTER VI
●●●●●●●●●●●●●●●●●●●●●●●●

PRINTERS

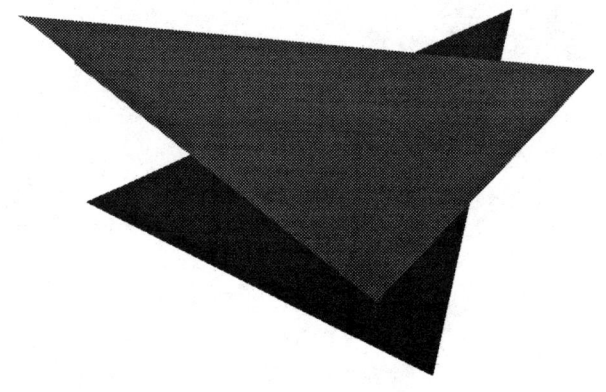

Paper Sources

ACI/Action Communications
612/636-3559

Atlantic Papers
PO Box 1158, Lemont, PA 16851
800/367-8547

Bandelier Designs Inc.
2504 Camino Entrada, Santa Fe, NM 87505
800/727-3792   505/474-0900

Collage
PO Box 7216, San Francisco, CA 94120-7216
800/9-COLLAGE

Conservatree Paper Co
1541 Adrian Rd, Burlingame, CA 94010
800/233-5335

Dancing Colors Papers
PO Box 416, Folsom, CA 95763
916/985-7116

Earth Care Paper Inc
PO Box 8007, Ukiah, CA 95482
800/347-0070

Elinor Eisemann
6520 Overhill Rd, Shawnee Mission, KS 66208
913/236-9824
Hand-marbled papers.

Erica's Paper
1801 Fourth St, Berkeley, CA 94710
510/845-9530

Forestsaver
1860 Pond Rd, Ronkonkoma, NY 11779
800/777-9886
Envelopes, stationery, etc. made from recycled maps! Everyone opens these envelopes! They're great.

Goodstamps * Stampgoods
Keena KD Good
30901 Timberline Rd, Willits, CA 94390
800/637-6401

Grass Roots Paper Company
Denise DeMarie
322 NW 59th St, Newport, OR 97365
503/265-5288

Guy T Kuhn
31 S Potomac St, Hagerstown, MD 21740
800/833-9318   301/791-5768
Exciting papers from everywhere.

Image Street
800/IMAGE-ST

JC Paper
510/568-6604

Kaleidoscope Decorative Paper
PO Box 890063, Houston, TX 77289
713/488-1355

On Paper
800/820-2299

Paper Arts
Marie Kelzer
PO Box 14634, San Francisco, CA 94114
415/285-9127

Paper Direct
800/272-7377

Paper Source
232 W Chicago Ave, Chicago, IL 60610
312/337-0798

Paper Technologies
929 Calle Negocio #D, San Clemente, CA 92673
714/366-8799

Paper Zone
206/682-8644
Stores throughout Oregon and Washington/shipping nationwide.

Papers by Catherine
11726 N Marianne, Houston, TX 77071
713/723-3334
Handmade and decorative papers.

Premier Papers Inc
800/843-0414

Presentation Solutions
800/789-1331

Queblo/Stationery House
800/523-9080   800/638-3033

Printers

Paper Sources (cont.)

Robert Paper Co Inc
404 Park Ave S, New York, NY 10016
212/696-2640
Unusual greeting card stock.

Schleicher Hand-Marbled Paper
PO Box 1005, Weaverville, NC 28787
704/252-3155
Also have a video entitled "Experience the Magic of Marbling" for $34.45ppd.

Schoeller Papers
Box 250, Pulaski, NY 13142
315/298-5133
Greeting card stock.

Simpson Paper Co
9393 W 100th #500, Overland Park, KS 66210
913/451-6746
Greeting card stock.

Stephen Kinsella Fine Art Papers
PO Box 32420, St Louis, MO 63132
800/445-8865

Twinrocker Handmade Paper
PO Box 413, Brookston, IN 47923
317/563-3119

Wallis Artists' Materials
729 Bay St, Santa Cruz, CA 95060
800/429-1219

Whatman
Martin/F. Weber Co
2727 Southampton Rd, Philadelphia, PA 19154
Watercolor and print-making papers.

The Write Touch
5850 W 80th St, PO Box 68188, Indianapolis, IN 46268-0188
800/288-6824

Wyndstone Papers
1480 S Wolf Rd, Wheeling, IL 60090
708/537-9300

Pre-Press Services

Digital Color Services/Picture Conversion
703/998-5777

Envelope Sources

Mail-Well Envelopes
800/777-1204

Triangle Printing
PO Box 100854, 325 Hill Ave, Nashville, TN 37223
800/843-9529 615/254-1879
As low as $20 per 1000.

Publications

Conservatree's Greenline
10 Lombard St #200, San Francisco, CA 94111-1109
415/433-1000 ext 24
Has a quarterly newsletter and sells recycled papers.

Getting It Printed by Mark Beach
NADTP
PO Box 1020, Sewickly, PA 15143
800/435-7116 412/741-0609
Tells how to work effectively with printers to assure quality and schedule/$34.95 + shipping.

Paper Crafters
Rona Chumbook
6575 SW 86th Ave, Portland, OR 97223
503/223-0167
Great quarterly publication with extensive information on papers.

Papers for Printing: How to Choose the Right Paper at the Right Price for Any Printing Job by Mark Beach and Ken Russon
Coast to Coast Books
2934 NE 16th St, Portland, OR 97212

Which Paper? by Silvie Turner
Lyons & Burford
212/620-9580
A guide to choosing and using fine papers/ $26.95 + 2.50 shipping.

See pages 72-73 for more publications on Printmaking and Publishing.

Working With a Printer

Working with a printer can at times be frustrating as well as time-consuming. As you learn the lingo and understand your personal needs, it will become less and less frustrating.

There are some general things to keep in mind before you get something printed:

• Get at least 3 quotes (they are free). Often you will see a vast difference in prices. Sometimes this is due to the fact that the printer you are asking for a quote doesn't specialize in what you need or does not have the correct press for what you need.

• You can go to a local printer and look through their paper samples. Depending on what you are printing (a brochure, business card, stationery, flyer, etc.), ask the cost of their 'in-house' stock closest to the paper you like.

• Ask the printer for help with size requirements, i.e. if you make your piece just 1/2" smaller sometimes it can save on paper costs.

• Perhaps you can gang a four-color with someone else's.

• If you are doing a small print run (300-500 or less), it probably is more economical to photocopy it unless you want a certain color ink other than black. Instead of using colored ink, use colored paper.

• Request a proof sheet—you don't want undetected errors, and sometimes they are hard to find the first time around. Let a friend read it over for errors also.

• Don't rush your job or your printer—that's often when things go astray and your job looks like it!

• If you print 1000 postcards (generally 10 pt stock) in four-color, save out 500 that don't print on the second side, so they can be printed on the back at a different time.

• Posters are generally 70# stock.

• Separation costs need to be considered when doing four-color jobs. Sometimes the price is included in a quote, sometimes not!

Printers

The following printers are listed alphabetically by state. With the advent of fax machines and express deliveries, it is not necessary to deal with a clost-at-hand printer. Check out the prices of several printers before you make a decision. Midwest printers often have great priceson four-color printing.

❖ Kenyon Press
Larry Janisse
12616 Chadron Ave, Hawthorne, CA 90250
800/752-9395 310/331-4500
310/675-2358 Fax

Artists can call for a free brochure.
Our specialty is: Postcards
Year company was established: 1992
We have the following press:
One-color   Four-color
Our specialty is runs of:

500	1,000	5,000

We print:

Posters	Limited editions	Cards
Brochures	Flyers	Envelopes
Lithographs	Magazines	Menus

We offer these techniques:

Die-cuts	Embossing

Four -color posters/70# 24x36":

500 $2200	2000 $3100

Four-color postcards/10pt 4x6":

500 $360	2000 $500

❖ Post Script Press
Gary Herzoff
2861 Cypress St, Oakland, CA 94608
510/444-3934 510/444-2909 Fax

Artists can call for a free brochure.
Our specialty is: Postcards
Year company was established: 1992
We have the following press:
One-color   Two-color   Four-color
We print: Cards
Four-color postcards/12pt 4^1/4x5^1/4":

500 $150	1000 $200	2000 $350

Four-color postcards/12 pt 5^1/2x8^1/2":

500 $250	1000 $300	2000 $500

❖ Studio V
Juli Veee and Alexander Visnyei
4891 Biona Dr, San Diego, CA 92116
619/563-9009 521-0722 Fax

Our specialty is: Silkscreen
Year company was established: 1985
We have the following press: One-color
Our specialty is runs of: 500
We offer these techniques: Screen printing

❖ Serbin Communications
511 Olive St, Santa Barbara, CA 93101
800/876-6425 ext. 225

Artists can call for a free brochure.
Our specialty is: Postcards
We print:

Posters	Limited editions	Cards
Brochures	Flyers	Envelopes
Lithographs	Magazines	Books

Four-color postcards/10pt 4^1/16x5^1/16":

1250 $395	2500 $490

❖ Accurate Graphics
112 Main St, Norwalk, CT 06851
800/852-2005 203/847-4929
203/866-7011 Fax

Artists can call for a free brochure.
Specialty: Color seps and flyers
Four-color flyer/80# gloss enamel 4/4

1000 $378	2500 $470	5000 $623

❖ International Printing Access
Kenneth Clift
PO Box 705, Old Saybrook, CT 06475
203/388-0419 203/388-6754 Fax

Artists can call for a free brochure.
Our specialty is: Four-color postcards
Year company was established: 1990
We have the following press: Four-color
Our specialty is runs of: 500   1,000
We print:

Posters	Cards	Brochures
Flyers	Books	

We offer these techniques

Die-cuts	Embossing	Leaf stamping

Four-color posters/70# 24x36": 500 $2125
Four-color postcards/12pt 4x6":

500 $110	2000 $240

Our prices are very good, but our turn-around is rather slow. We have 6-8 print dates a year, and printing takes a further 6 weeks after that date.

❖ **Page Two Inc**
Tom Bannister
PO Box 77167, Washington, DC 20013
800/821-6604 802/538-7549 Fax

Artists can call for a free brochure.
Our specialty is: General business printing
Year company was established: 1981
We have the following press:
One-color   Two-color
Our specialty is runs of:
500   1,000   5,000
We print:
Cards   Brochures   Flyers
Envelopes   Newsletters   Labels
Notepads   Computer forms
We offer these techniques:
Die-cuts   Embossing   Thermography

❖ **National Art Reproductions**
11555 Marshwood Ln, Ft Myers, FL 33908
800/769-6270 813/466-5999 Fax

Four-color posters/80# cover 18xz23":
500 $1195 1000 $1349
Four-color posters/80# cover 16x20":
500 $1075 1000 $1199

❖ **US Press**
PO Box 640, Valdosta, GA 31603-0640
800/227-7377

Artists can call for a free brochure.
Our specialty is: Postcards
Four-color postcards/12pt 4x6":
5000 $435   10,000 $655

❖ **Saltzman Printers Inc**
Jack Saltzman
50 Madison St, Maywood, IL 60153
800/952-2800 708/344-4500
708/344-9423 Fax

Artists can call for a free brochure.
Our specialty is: Color brochures
Year company was established: 1946
We have the following press:
One-color   Two-color   Four-color
Our specialty is runs of:
1,000   5,000   25,000
We print:
Posters   Limited editions Cards
Brochures   Flyers   Lithographs
Books

We offer these techniques:
Die-cuts   Embossing
Four-color posters/70# 24x36" (from film):
500 $1250   2000 $2200
Four-color postcards/10pt 4x6" (from film):
500 $595   2000 $695

❖ **Multi Print Co Inc**
Monica Pratl
5555 W Howard St, Skokie, IL 60077
800/858-9999 708/677-7544 Fax

Artists can call for a free brochure.
Our specialty is: Four-color
Year company was established: 1932
We have the following press:
Two-color   Four-color   Seven-color
Our specialty is runs of:
500   1,000   5,000
25,000
We print:
Posters   Limited editions Cards
Brochures   Flyers   Lithographs
We offer these techniques:
Die-cuts   Embossing
Four-color posters/90# (Eloquence) 24x36":
500 $1365   2000 $1830
Four-color postcards/10pt 4x6" (includes seps):
500 $555   2000 $599
Complete desktop publishing capabilities in-house with a full-service art department. Also provide color seps and a bindery in one location.

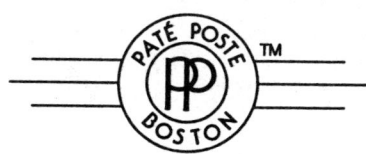

❖ **Paté Poste**
Marvin Getman
43 Charles St, Boston, MA 02114
800/356-0002 617/720-2855
617/723-7683 Fax

Year company was established: 1985
We have the following press: Four-color
Our specialty is runs of: 1,000
We print:
Posters   Limited editions Cards
Brochures   Flyers   Lithographs
We offer these techniques: Prints to canvas

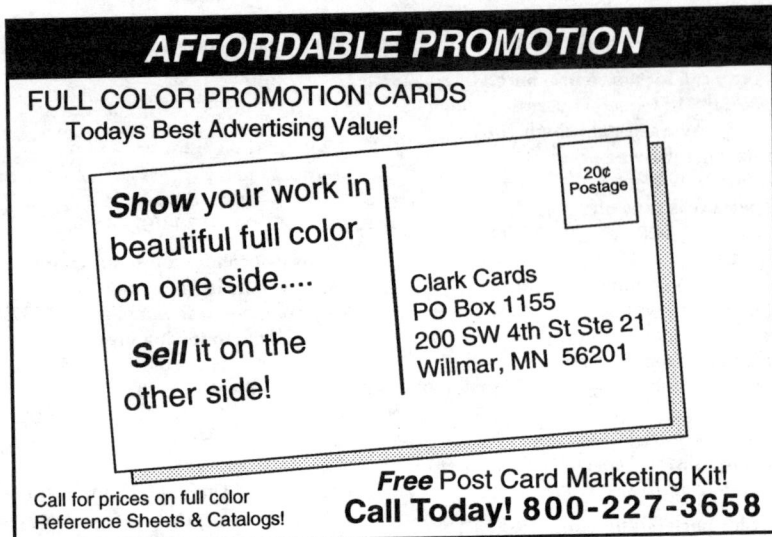
❖ **Watt/Peterson Inc**
Bruce A Warner, VP Sales & Marketing
15020 27th Ave N, Plymouth, MN 55447
800/328-3328 612/553-1617
612/553-0956 Fax

Our specialty is: Four-color sheetfed printing
Year company was established: 1963
We have the following press: Four-color
We print:

Posters   Limited editions Cards
Brochures   Books   Calendars
Promotional materials

❖ **Clark Cards**
Dennis Clark
PO Box 1155, 200 SW 4th St #21, Willmar,
MN 56201
800/227-3658 612/231-3309
612/231-1472 Fax

Artists can call for a free brochure.
Our specialty is: Promotion cards
Year company was established: 1990
We have the following press: Four-color
We print:
Cards   Brochures   Flyers
Catalogs

84

❖ C&W Printing
Jacqui Walker
1431 Washington Blvd #2411, Detroit, MI 48226
313/965-2834 313/965-2834 Fax

Artists can call for a free brochure.
Year company was established: 1994
We have the following press:
One-color Two-color Four-color
Our specialty is runs of:
500 1,000 5,000
25,000
We print:
Posters Limited editions Cards
Brochures Flyers Envelopes
Lithographs Magazines Books
Business cards
We offer these techniques:
Embossing Thermography Leaf stamping
Holograms Silkscreen
Four-color posters/70# 24x36" (Seps separate): 2000 $2975
Four-color postcards/10pt 4x6" (Seps separate): 500 $275 2000 $350
Fax request for quote; reply within 24 hours.

❖ Mitchell Graphics Inc
Jamie Winters
2363 Mitchell Park Dr, Petoskey, MI 49770
800/583-9401 616/347-4635
616/347-9255 Fax

Artists can call for a free brochure.
Our specialty is: Four-color
Year company was established: 1972
We have the following press:
Two-color Four-color
Our specialty is runs of:
1,000 5,000 25,000
We print:
Posters Cards Brochures
Flyers Fine art prints
We offer these techniques: Die-cuts

❖ Unity Screen Printing and Tiles
Layah Cottonwood
786 E Reserve Dr, Kalispell, MT 59901
406/257-5056

Our specialty is: Custom designed tiles, posters, banners and signs, screen printing
Year company was established: 1990
Our specialty is runs of: 500
We print:
Posters Limited editions Tiles
Banners Signs

❖ Dynamic Impressions
130 Maple St, Friend, NE 68359
800/342-8282 402/947-2391
402/947-3631 Fax

Artists can call for a free brochure.
Our specialty is: Postcards/posters
Year company was established: 1988
We have the following press:
One-color Four-color
We print:
Posters Cards Brochures
Flyers Envelopes Books
Letterhead Pads Office forms
Four-color postcards/15pt 4x6":
2500 $330 5000 $440

❖ Show & Tell Communications
Mark Thellmann
PO Box 1209, Merchantville, NJ 08109
609/488-9093 ext. 23 for fax

Artists can call for a free brochure.
Our specialty is: Postcards to posters
Year company was established: 1985
We have the following press: Four-color
Our specialty is runs of: 1,000+
We print:
Posters Cards Brochures
Flyers Greeting cards Business cards
Art reproductions
We offer these techniques:
Die-cuts Embossing Prints to canvas

❖ Challenge Graphics Services Inc
Sheldon Morgan
18 Connor Ln, Deer Park, NY 11729
800/242-5364 516/586-0171
516/586-0174 Fax

Artists can call for a free brochure.
Our specialty is: Artist reprint sheets
Year company was established: 1975
We have the following press: Six-color
We print:
Posters Limited editions Cards
Brochures Flyers Lithographs
Books
We offer these techniques:
Die-cuts Embossing Leaf stamping
Four-color posters/80# 24x36":
2500 $2900
Four-color postcards/10pt 4x6":
2500 $325

Printers

❖ Ken Lieberman Laboratories Inc
Ken Lieberman
118 W 22 St, New York, NY 10011
212/633-0500 212/675-8269 Fax

Artists can call for a free brochure.
Our specialty is: Custom prints
Year company was established: 1975
We print: Limited editions
We offer these techniques:
Prints to canvas/custom photographic prints
copied from paintings

❖ Flower City Printing Inc
Mark Ashworth
4800 Dewey Ave, PO Box 12590, Rochester,
NY 14612
800/444-4832 716/663-9000
716/663-4908 Fax

Artists can call for a free brochure.
Our specialty is: High quality
Year company was established: 1970
We have the following press:
Two-color   Four-color
Our specialty is runs of:
5,000   25,000
We print:
Posters   Limited editions Cards
Brochures   Flyers   Envelopes
Lithographs Books
We offer these techniques: Die-cuts

❖ Art Press
Julia Gibson/Customer Service
8125 Uehling Ln, Dayton, OH 45424
800/833-2961 513/237-8211
513/237-8210 Fax

Artists can call for a free brochure.
Our specialty is: Fine art reproductions
Year company was established: 1990
We have the following press:
One-color   Two-color   Four-color
Our specialty is runs of: 500
We print:
Posters   Limited editions Cards
Brochures   Flyers   Lithographs
Books
**Four-color posters/100# offset enamel
24x36":**
500 $1800   2000 $2880
Four-color postcards/10pt 4x6":
500 $210   2000 $400

❖ Color Q
Cathy Humphries
2710 Dryden Rd, Dayton, OH 45439
800/999-1007 513/294-0406
513/294-8896 Fax

Artists can call for a free brochure.
We have the following press:
One-color   Two-color   Four-color
Our specialty is runs of: 100
We print:
Posters   Limited editions Cards
Brochures   Flyers
We offer these techniques: Prints to canvas
Four-color posters/80# 24x36":
500 $2035   2000 $3205
Four-color postcards/10pt 4x6":
500 $275   2000 $470

❖ Quality Color
Michael Hipp
1000 Conger St, Eugene, OR 97405
800/688-4741 503/484-4741
503/344-0572 Fax

We have the following press: Four-color
Our specialty is runs of: 1,000
We print:
Posters   Cards   Brochures
Flyers   Envelopes
We offer these techniques:
Die-cuts   Embossing
Four-color posters/70# 24x18":
500 $1027   2000 $2356
Four-color postcards/10pt 4x6":
500 $365   2000 $390

Art Editions

❖ **Art Editions**
Ruby Reece
352 W Paxton Ave, Salt Lake City, UT
84101
800/331-8449 801/466-6088
801/485-5250 Fax

Artists can call for a free brochure.
Our specialty is: Fine art printing
Year company was established: 1984
We have the following press:
One-color   Four-color
Our specialty is runs of:

1,000	5,000	25,000

We print:

Posters	Cards	Brochures
Flyers	Envelopes	Limited editions

All types of fine art
We also produce art folios for prints.
We offer these techniques:

Die-cuts	Embossing	Engraving
Leaf stamping		

❖ **Keeper Kard**
225 164th St SE #103, Bothell, WA 98012
800/929-5361 206/743-8895

Artists can call for a free brochure.
Our specialty is: Postcards
Year company was established: 1992
We have the following press: Four-color
Our specialty is runs of:

1,000	2500

We offer these techniques

Die-cuts	Embossing

Four-color postcards/10pt 4x6":

500 $225	2500 $350

❖ **Glatt & Tmagos**
Mary Kamimura
Rua Francsico Leita 116, Jardim America,
Sao Paulo, Brasil
011/853-3188 011/280-7289 Fax

Our specialty is: Producing and distributing prints
We print:

Lithographs	Serigraphs	Etchings

We offer:
Brokers, dealers and wholesalers for our products

CHAPTER VII
●●●●●●●●●●●●●●●●●●●●●●●●

ORGANIZATIONS

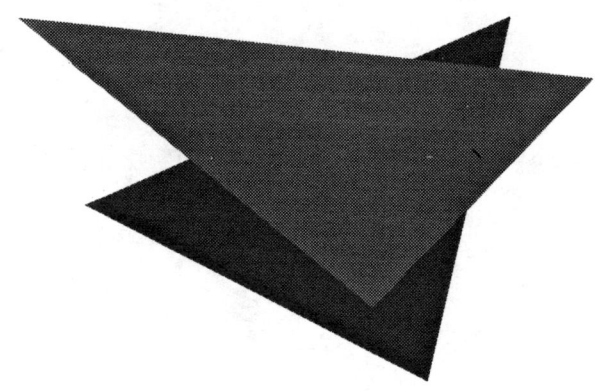

National Art Organizations

American Art Therapy Association
Nancy Knapp
1202 Allanson Rd, Mundelein, IL 60060
708/949-6064

American Arts Alliance
Anne Murphy
1319 F St NW #307, Washington, DC 20004
202/737-1727

American Association of Museums
Jeff Minet
1225 Eye St, Washington, DC 20005
202/289-1818

American Craft Council
40 W 53rd St, New York, NY 10019
212/956-3535
Slide registry.

American Federation of Arts
41 E 65th St, New York, NY 10021
212/988-7700

American Institute of Architects/AIA
1735 New York Ave NW, Washington, DC 20006
202/626-7300

American Physicians Art Association
307 2nd Ave, New York, NY 10003

American Society of Interior Designers/ASID
Robert Angle
608 Massachusetts Ave NE, Washington, DC 20002-6006
202/546-3480

Art & Antique Dealers League of America
David Dava
1020 Madison Ave, New York, NY 10021
212/879-7558

Art Dealers Association of America
Donna Carlson
575 Madison Ave, New York, NY 10022
212/940-8590

Art for a Better Image/ArtFBI
Jeff Gates
2000 Hermitage Ave, Silver Springs, MD 20902
301/949-0436
Arts advocacy information and opportunities/ on-line/$30 per year.

Art Information Center
189 Lexington Ave, New York, NY 10016
212/227-0282
Slide registry.

ARTS
Joy Fuller
315 W Ninth St #201, Los Angeles, CA 90015
213/627-9276
Assists in strengthening and supporting non-profit arts organizations in Southern California.

Association of Art Museum Directors
PO Box 10082, Savannah, GA 31402
404/234-1393

Association of Corporate Art Advisors
544 W Queen Ln, Philadelphia, PA 19144
215/848-5791

Association of Corporate Art Curators
Box 11369, Chicago, IL 60611-0369
414/229-6243

Association of Professional Art Advisors/APAA
2150 W 29th Ave #500, Denver, CO 80211
303/433-4446

California Assembly of Local Art Agencies/ CALAA
870 Market St #714, San Francisco, CA 94102-2902
415/775-7200

City of Brea
Emily Sabin
1 Civic Center Cir, Brea, CA 92621
714/990-7713
Slide registry.

Club of American Collectors of Fine Arts
Jacques Athias
20 W 64th St #21K, New York, NY 10023
212/769-1860

College Art Association/CAA
275 7th Ave, New York, NY 10001

Organizations

National Art Organizations (cont.)

Combined Organizations for the Visual Arts/ COVA
744 G St #202A, San Diego, CA 92101
619/234-0928

Commission on Arts & Humanities
1111 E Street NW #B500, Washington, DC 20004
202/724-5613

Committee for the Visual Arts
Artspace
223 W Broadway, New York, NY 10013
212/226-3970
Slide registry.

Connecticut Commission on the Arts
227 Lawrence St, Hartford, CT 06106
Slide registry.

Copley Society of Boston
158 Newbury St, Boston, MA 02116
617/536-5049
Slide registry.

Curatorial Assistance
113 E Union St, Los Angeles, CA 91103
213/681-2401

Gallery Association of New York State
Box 345 Hamilton, NY 13346
315/824-2510

General Services Administration
Art in Architecture Program
18th & F Sts NW, #1300, Washington, DC 20405
202/566-0950
Slide registry.

Guild of Natural Science Illustrators
PO Box 652, Ben Franklin Station, Washington, DC 20044

Independent Curators Inc
799 Broadway #205, New York, NY 10003
212/254-8200

International Confederation of Art Dealers
32 E 57th, New York, NY 10022

International Sculpture Center
1050 Potomac St NW, Washington, DC 20007
202/965-6066
Slide registry.

International Society of Copier Artists
800 West End Ave, New York, NY 10025
212/662-5533

Los Angeles County Transportation Commission
818 W 7th St #1100, Los Angeles, CA 90017
213/244-6408
Slide registry.

Mid-America Arts Exhibit
James Olson
912 Baltimore Ave #700, Kansas City, MO 64105
816/421-3918

National Antique & Art Dealers Association
32 E 57th St, New York, NY 10022
212/355-0636

National Art Dealers Association of America
Mark Acoby
12 E 56th St, New York, NY 10022-3104
212/826-9707

National Assembly of Local Arts Agencies/ NALAA
927 15th St NW 12Fl, Washington, DC 20005
Provides percent-for-art information for local projects.

National Assembly of State Arts Agencies
1010 Vermont Ave NW, Washington, DC 20005
202/347-6352
Provides a current list of percent-for-art programs.

National Association of Artist's Organizations/ NAAO
Charlotte Murphy
918 F St NW #611, Washington, DC 20004
202/347-6350

National Association of Corporate Art Management
SS Wenegrat
PO Box 78 Church Street Station, New York, NY 10008
212/435-3397 212/435-3382 Fax
Non-profit arts organization that has a newsletter entitled "NACAM."

National Association of Educators in the Arts/ NAEA
1916 Association Dr, Reston, VA 22091
703/860-8000

National Association of Schools of Art & Design
George Bayliss
11250 Roger Bacon Dr #5, Reston, VA 22090
703/437-0700

National Campaign For Freedom of Expression
1402 3rd Ave #421, Seattle, WA 98101
206/340-9301

National Endowment for the Arts/NEA
1100 Pennsylvania Ave NW #729, Washington, DC 20506
202/682-5448

National Expressive Therapy Association
Steve Ross
1164 Bishop St #124, Honolulu, HI 96813
808/524-5411

National Neon Institute
Lee Champagne
1070 Tyler St, Benicia, CA 94510
707/747-6167

National Society of Minority Writers & Artists
Doris Kwasikpuk
PO Box 3424, Greensboro, NC 27402

New England Art Therapy Institute
Meg Heisse
216 S Silver Ln, Sunderland, MA 01375
413/665-4880

New England Artists' Registry/NEAR
Barbara Green
Box 165, Housatonic, MA 01236
Non-profit slide registry, computerized and cross-referenced for New England artists.

New Museum
137 Greene St, New York, NY 10012
212/219-1355
Slide registry.

NY Viewing Room
101 Wooster, New York, NY 10012
Slide registry.

Public Art Fund
1285 Ave of the Americas 3Fl, New York, NY 10019
Slide registry.

Society for Non-Profit Organizations
6314 Odana Rd #1, Madison, WI 53719
608/274-9777

Society of Professional Artists Reps/SPAR
60 E 42nd St #1166, New York, NY 10651
212/779-7464

Southern Arts Federation
1811 14th St NE #400, Atlanta, GA 30309
404/874-7244

State of New Mexico
228 E Palace Ave, Santa Fe, NM 87501
505/827-6490
Slide registry.

Studio Space/Sculpture Space
Sylvia de Swain
12 Gates St, Utica, NY 13502
315/724-8381
Slide registry.

Support Center for Non-Profit Management
70 Tenth St #201, San Francisco, CA 94103
415/874-7244

Vietnam Veterans Artists Alliance
Rob Watkins
PO Box 1153, Land O'Lakes, FL 33539
305/949-3457

Visual Artists and Galleries Association/VAGA
1 Rockefeller Plz #2626, New York, NY 10020
212/397-8353

Organizations

National Art Organizations (cont.)

Visual Arts Office
Oregon Arts Commission
550 Airport Rd SE, Salem, OR 97310
503/378-3625
Slide registry.

Washington Project for the Arts
Jock Reynolds
400 7th St NW, Washington, DC 20004
202/347-4813

International Art Organizations

ANNPAC/RACA
Ric Amis
183 Bathurst St, Main Fl, Toronto, Ontario,
Canada M5T 2R7
416/869-1275

Artist's League of Great Britain
Bankside Gallery
48 Hopton St, London, England SE1 9JH

Arts
40 Dover St, London, England W1X 3RB

Arts Council of Great Britain
105 Piccadilly, London, England W1V OAU

Association of Artistes Ontarios
Boite 824, Chatham, Ontario, Canada

Federation of British Artists
17 Carlton House Ter, London, England
SW1Y 5BD

National Association for the Visual Arts
Anna Ward
The Gunnery, 43-51 Cowper Wharf Rd,
Woolloomooloo, Australia NSW 2011
02/318-1600

National Society of Art Education
71 High St, Corsham, Wilshire, England
SN13 OES

Very Special Art Programs

Americans with Disabilities Act
800/514-0301
This federal legislation began in 1992 and affects business employing people. For technical support and grant information.

Citizens for Special Artists
610 Brazos 4Fl, Austin, TX 78701

Deaf Artists of America/DAA
Tom Willard
87 N Clinton Ave #408, Rochester, NY 14604
716/325-2403

Enabled Artists' Guild
PO Box 4537, Salem, OR 97302-8537
503/769-7454

Enabled Artists United
PO Box 178, Dobbins, CA 95935
916/692-1581
Has a newsletter.

Epilepsy Society of New York City
305 7th Ave 12Fl, New York, NY 10001
212/633-2930
Curator of the annual art show for artists with disabilities.

Expressions
Serendipity Press
PO Box 16294, St Paul, MN 55116
612/451-1208
Semi-annual magazine featuring artists with disabilities. Send SASE for guidelines.

Handicapped Activities Unltd
511 Grand Ave, Pacific Grove, CA 93950

National Art & Disabilities
Bobbie Altman
551 23rd St, Richmond, CA 94804
510/620-0290

National Exhibits by Blind Artists/NEBA
919 Walnut St, Philadelphia, PA 19107
215/627-0600 ext 296

UCPSH
Cheryl Haltman
326 Locust St, Akron, OH 44302-1876
216/379-3349TDD
Features a magazine entitled "Kaleidoscope: International Magazine of Literature, Fine Arts and Disability."

Very Special Arts AZ
Carroll Rinehart
3321 N Chapel Ave, Tucson, AZ 85716
520/795-6502

Very Special Arts DC
Stephanie Smutz
1331 F St NW, Washington, DC 20004
202/628-0800

Very Special Arts Gallery
Denise Warner
1300 Connecticut Ave NW, Washington, DC 20036
202/628-0800 202/737-0725 Fax
Has a gallery with competitions as well as a store and newsletter. Also has a slide registry and art library.

Very Special Arts MI
821 W Eleven Mile Rd, Royal Oak, MI 48067
313/546-9298

Very Special Arts MN
Hennepin Center For The Arts
528 Hennepin Ave #201, Minneapolis, MN 55403
612/332-3888

Very Special Arts MS
PO Box 5365, Mississippi State, MS 39762
601/325-2367

Very Special Arts MO
Behavioral Studies Department
8001 Natural Bridge Rd, Saint Louis, MO 63121
314/553-5752

Very Special Arts MT
U of M
25 N Corbin Hall, Missoula, MT 59812
406/243-4847

Organizations

Very Special Art Programs (cont.)

Very Special Arts NE
PO Box 163, Norfolk, NE 68702-0163
402/887-5444

Very Special Arts NV
Mary Ellen Horan
200 Flint St, Reno, NV 89501
702/329-1401

Very Special Arts NH
80 N Main St 2Fl, Concord, NH 03301-4942
603/228-4330

Very Special Arts NJ
841 Georges Rd, North Brunswick, NJ 08902
908/745-3885

Very Special Arts NM
Beth Rudolph
PO Box 7784, 2015 Yale Blvd SE,
Albuquerque, NM 87106
505/766-9620 505/245-8545
Has gallery space, sponsors competitive exhibitions, holds residencies, sponsors seminars and has a newsletter "Arts Access," edited by Lisa Huey.

Very Special Arts NY
18-05 215th St, Flushing, NY 11360
718/225-6305

Very Special Arts NY
Margaret Chapman School
5 Bradhurst Ave, Hawthorne, NY 10532
914/592-8526

Very Special Arts NC
Division of Exceptional Childrens Services
301 Wilmington St, Raleigh, NC 27601-1058
919/715-1597
Has a gallery and competitive exhibitions as well as sponsoring of classes and seminars.

Very Special Arts OH
Baker & Hostetler
65 E State S #2100, Columbus, OH 43215
614/462-4715

Very Special Arts OK
PO Box 54490, Oklahoma City, OK 73154
405/948-6411

Very Special Arts OR
PO Box 304, Salem, OR 97308-0304
503/378-3598

Very Special Arts PA
117 Tuscarora St, Harrisburg, PA 17104
717/238-0907

Very Special Arts RI
500 Prospect St, Pawtucket, RI 02860
401/725-0247

Very Special Arts SC
PO Box 575, Ladson, SC 29456
803/821-5849

Very Special Arts SD
301 S Garfield Ave #8, Sioux Falls, SD 57104
605/339-4393

Very Special Arts TN
6431 Tea Rose Ter, Brentwood, TN 37027
615/373-8420

Very Special Arts TX
18383 Gallery Dr, Dallas, TX 75252
214/732-1179

Very Special Arts UT
PO Box 52644, Salt Lake City, UT 84152
801/328-0703

Very Special Arts VT
PO Box 432, Winooski, VT 05404-0432
802/655-4105

Very Special Arts VA
PO Box 29081, Richmond, VA 23229
804/225-2070

Very Special Arts WA
158 Thomas St #15, Seattle, WA 98109
206/443-1843

Very Special Arts WV
Marshall U
400 Hal Greer Blvd, Huntington, WV 25755
304/696-6384

Very Special Arts WI
4797 Hayes Rd #202, Madison, WI 53704
608/241-2131

Very Special Arts WY
6009 Horse Creek Rd, Cheyenne, WY 82009
307/634-8812

Acrylic Organizations

National Society of Painters in Acrylic
Mark Freeman
32 Union Square East #1214, New York,
NY 10003

National Society of Painters in Acrylic
Douglas Wiltrout
969 Catasaqua Rd, Whitehall, PA 18052
215/264-7472

Bamboo Organization

American Bamboo Society
321 S Main St #508, Sebastopol, CA 95472

Experimental Organization

Society of Experimental Artists
Gracie Hegeman
PO Box 10929, Bradenton, FL 34282

Layerists Organization

Society of Layerists in Multi-Media
Mary Nelson
1408 Georgia NE, Albuquerque, NM 87110
505/268-1100

Oil Organizations

National Oil & Acrylic Painters Society
Richard Monson
PO Box 676, Osage Beach, MO 65065
Sponsors competitive exhibitions and has a newsletter.

Oil Painters of America
Shirl Smithson
601 S Lincoln Ave, Park Ridge, IL 60068
708/823-5384

Pencil Organizations

Colored Pencil Society of America
Kay Dewar
3056 39 SW, Seattle, WA 98116

Colored Pencil Society of America/CPA
4760 Andette Ave NW, Massillion, OH
44647

Organizations

Pastel Societies

Arizona Pastel Artists Association
Ruth Palmisano
6231 W Monterey Wy, Phoenix, AZ 85033
602/247-3877

Ozark Pastel Society
Cheryl Netherton
PO Box 95, Maysville, AR 72747
918/529-4441

Pastel Society of the West Coast
1250 Grizzly Flat Ct, Auburn, CA 95603
916/885-7223
Conducts competitive exhibitions, gives scholarships,"PSWC Newsletter," edited by Suzanne Blaney, holds classes and seminars, has an art library.

Pastel Society of the West Coast
PO Box 1032, Diamond Springs, CA 95619

Pastel Society of San Diego
Jack Nicholson
PO Box 80523, Central PO, San Diego, CA 92138-0523

Connecticut Pastel Society
Madelaine Moriarty
53 Colony Rd, Meriden, CT 06450

Florida Pastel Association
3943 Riverview Blvd W, Bradenton, FL 34209

Pastel Society of North Florida
PO Box 5133, Fort Walton Beach, FL 32549

Southeastern Pastel Society
Virginia Munroe
2906 Templar Knight Dr, Tucker, GA 30084
404/493-8749
They sponsor competitive exhibitions, have a slide registry and a newsletter "Dustbuster," edited by Mikki Dillon.

Midwest Pastel Society
David McElroy
6343 N Claremont, Chicago, IL 60693
312/761-6136
Sponsors competitions, seminars and has a newsletter "Pastel Paper," edited Carrie Czarlew.

Kansas Pastel Society
Barbara Scott
PO Box 8122, Wichita, KS 67208

Degas Pastel Society
D Johnson
3950 S Pine Oak Ave, New Orleans, LA 70131

Maryland Pastel Society
Betty Knight
PO Box 54, Riderwood, MD 21139
301/467-6748

Kalamazoo Area Pastel Society
Carol Higedus
4867 Fox Fire Tr, Kalamazoo, MI 49009

Cassatt Pastel Society
Sandra Place
Rte 3 Box 109D, Santa Fe, NM 87505
505/984-0160

Pastel Society of America
Sidney Hermel
15 Gramercy Park Sq, New York, NY 10003
212/533-6931

Oil Pastel Association
John Elliot
PO Box 587, Nyack, NY 10960
914/353-2483

Pastel Society of Oregon
Jody Batson
PO Box 105, Roseburg, OR 97470
503/672-0572

Pastel Society of the Southwest
Beverly Boren
2248 Big Bend, Carrollton, TX 75007

Pastel Society of the Southwest
Vicky Kuykendall
PO Box 670841, Dallas, TX 75367-0841
214/352-8246 (Dorothy Barta)

Pastel Society of the West Coast
Adele Lloyd
2603 78th Ave NE, Bellevue, WA 98004

Northwest Pastel Society
Peggy Braeutigon
1420 NW Gilman Blvd #2732, Issaquah, WA 98027-7001
206/285-6005

Watercolor Organizations

Watercolor Society of Alabama
Ophelia Massey
PO Box 43011, Birmingham, AL 35223

Watercolor Society of Alabama
Cathy Moeller
Rte 13 Box 154A, Florence, AL 35630

Alaska Watercolor Society
PO Box 90714, Anchorage, AK 99502
907/349-4047
AKWS /Henry Yuen, Editor

Mid-Southern Watercolorists
Reita Walker-Miller
57 Tallyho Ln W 3Fl, Little Rock, AR 72207

Arizona Watercolor Association
Rod Zohner
PO Box 37071, Phoenix, AZ 85069
602/943-2626
Pam Zohner, Editor

Contemporary Watercolorists of Arizona
Garnette Widdifield
3313 E Onyx Ave, Phoenix, AZ 85028

Arizona Watercolor Association
Bette Hedblam
13319 Castle Rock Dr, Sun City West, AZ 85375
602/279-6354

Southern Arizona Watercolor Guild
Louise Wyant
1881 North King St, Tucson AZ 85749

Santa Cruz County Watercolor Society
Melita Israel
1970 Cox Rd, Aptos, CA 95003

West Coast Watercolor Society
149 Hawthorn Dr, Atherton, CA 94027

Watercolor Artists of Sacramento
6101 Winding Wy, Carmichael, CA 95608

National Watercolor Society
John Salchak
18220 S Hoffman Ave, Cerritos, CA 90701

National Watercolor Society
Phyllis Solcyk
20223 Labrador, Chatsworth, CA 91311
818/349-4296
Newsletter.

National Watercolor Society
Willellyn McFarland
7937 E Fourth Pl, Downey, CA 90241

National Watercolor Society
Elaine Harvey
1602 Sunburst Dr, El Cajon, CA 91006

Westcoast Watercolor Society
Ken Siqueira
1035 Contra Costa Dr, El Cerrito, CA 94530

Watercolor West
2943 Sunny Crest Dr #400, Fullerton, CA 92635

Marin County Watercolor Society
Ellan Gannon
364 Via Casitas, Greenbrae, CA 94904

National Watercolor Society
Mark Florian
605 West Rd, La Habra, Heights, CA 90631

National Watercolor Society
Joan Fey
3511 Manhattan Ave, Manhattan Beach, CA 90266

National Watercolor Society
Joe Carmichael
985 San Pasqual, Pasadena, CA 91106

Monterey Peninsula Watercolor Society
Margaret Roberts
PO Box 793, Pebble Beach, CA 93953

Watercolor West
Pat Fullerton
PO Box 213, Redlands, CA 92373

NWS
Mary Lind
517 N Prospect Ave, Redondo Beach, CA 90277

California Watercolor Workshops Ltd
Patricia Abraham
3334 Lowther Way, Sacramento, CA 95842

Organizations

Watercolor Organizations (cont.)

San Diego Watercolor Society
Elaine Harvey
5651 Raymar Ave, San Diego, CA 92021

Eastbay Watercolor Society
Kathie Boissiere
767 Widgeon St, San Mateo, CA 94404
415/573-1889

Delta Watercolor Society
Maxine White
1417 N Edison St, Stockton, CA 95203

Santa Clara Valley Watercolor Society
Addie Johnson
713 Gail Avenue, Sunnyvale, CA 94086

Valley Watercolor Society
Ann Gross
5066 Veloz Ave, Tarzana, CA 91356

Eastbay Watercolor Society
PO Box 4631, Walnut Creek, CA 94596

Colorado Watercolor Society
Ed Brookins
2219 S Joliet Wy, Aurora, CO 80014
303/743-8827
"Collage," edited by Judy Gunther.

Broadmoor Watercolour Society
Georgia Edmondson
1034-C Fontmore Rd, Colorado Springs, CO
80904
719/633-3481

Colorado Watercolor Workshop
Nancy Baldrica
3305 Brenner Pl, Colorado Springs, CO
80917
719/591-0380

Pikes Peak Watercolor Society
Gwen Fox
2017 Brookwood Dr, Colorado Springs, CO
80918

Western Colorado Watercolor
Wilda Fortune
1907 N 3rd Ct, Grand Junction, CO 81501

Connecticut Watercolor Society
Nancy Greene
PO Box 486, Farmington, CT 06034

American Watercolor Society
Richard Brzozowski
23 Fox Rd, Plainville, CT 06062

Palm Beach Watercolor Society
Carol Wedin
PO Box 1916, Boca Raton, FL 33429

Florida Suncoast Watercolor Society
Lee Mears
7612 18th Ave NW, Bradenton, FL 34209

Florida Watercolor Society
Richard French
2152 Imperial Point Dr, Ft Lauderdale, FL
33308

Jacksonville Watercolor Society
Miles Batt
2739 Algonquin Ave, Jacksonville, FL 32210

Citrus Watercolor Club
Ray Jowers
PO Box 142, Lecanto, FL 34460

Miami Watercolor Society
Gudrun Napp
PO Box 561953, Miami, FL 33156-1953
305/361-6016
*"MWS Newsletter," edited by Ana Lorena Quiros;
has juried membership competitions, workshops,
and a color-copy slide registry.*

Tallahassee Watercolor Society
Rosemary Ferguson
PO Box 38502, Tallahassee, FL 32315
904/386-1693
Newsletter/Jim Grosvenor, Editor

Southern Watercolor Society
Annette Bush
202 Greene St, Augusta, GA 30901

Georgia Watercolor Society
Carolynn Mann
1475 Jones Rd, Roswell, GA 30075

Hawaii Watercolor Society
Gig Greenwood
PO Box 22404, Honolulu, HI 96823

Organizations

Iowa Watercolor Society
Jo Myers-Walcker
2304 Storm St, Ames, IA 50010

Idaho Watercolor Society
Ed Lahadil
PO Box 9093, Boise, ID 83707-3093

Illinois Watercolor Society
Myrle Howell
PO Box 482, Glenview, IL 60025

Lakes Region Watercolor Society
Patricia Wylie
1545 Willow St, Lake Forest, IL 60045

Great River Watercolor Society
1515 Jersey St, Quincy, IL 62301

Watercolor Society of Indiana
Carolyn Johnson
11054 Spring Mill Ln, Carmel, IN 46032

Wabash Valley Watercolor Society
Mary Ann Spitznagle
5502 E 400 N, Lafayette, IN 47905-9770

Kansas Watercolor Society
Ruth Sanderson
PO Box 1796, Hutchinson, KS 67504
316/722-6007
"KWS News," edited by Sharon Connaway.

Northern Kentucky Watercolor Society
Beulah Chapin
1324 Old State Rd, Covington, KY 41011

Kentucky Watercolor Society
Aline Barker
PO Box 7125, Louisville, KY 40207-1025

Louisiana Watercolor Society
Karen Jacobs
53 Belle Grove, Destrehan, LA 70047

New Iberia Watercolor Society
Arthur Tomlinson
143 W Main St, New Iberia, LA 70560

Louisiana Watercolor Society
Bill McInnis
PO Box 870581, New Orleans, LA 70127
"Waterworks," edited by Susan Copping; sponsors classes and competitive exhibitions.

Potomac Valley Watercolorists
Lesley McCaskill
9705 Singleton Dr, Bethesda, MD 20817

Washington Water Color Assoc
Doris Stade
48808 Moorland Ln, Bethesda, MD 20814

Baltimore Watercolor Society
Alice Webb
4700 Centennial Ln, Ellicott City, MD 20143

Potomac Valley Watercolorists
Yolanda Frederikse
9625 Dewmar Ln, Kensington, MD 20895

Boston Society of Watercolor Painters
Mary Jo Rines
162 Newbury St, Boston, MA 02116
617/893-5582

New England Watercolor Society
Nancy Howell
91 Scott Cir, Dedham, MA 02026

Midwest Watercolor Society
Mary Ann Beckwith
619 Lake Ave, Hancock, MI 49930

Michigan Watercolor Society
Fran Waring
PO Box 99344, Troy, MI 48099-9344

Twin Cities Watercolor Society
Mariann Alstad
3949 11th Ave S, Minneapolis, MN 55407
612/824-6460

Central Minnesota Watercolorists
Sandy Piano
4315 Thru St, St Cloud, MN 56303

Northstar Watercolor Society
Judith Blain
2193 Deer Pass Tr, White Bear Lake, MN 55110
612/429-3453
Newsletter and sponsors classes.

Mississippi Watercolor Society
Sandra Williams
522 Robinhood Rd, Jackson, MS 39206

Organizations

Watercolor Organizations (cont.)

Watercolor USA
1111 E Brookside Dr, Springfield, MO 65807

Montana Watercolor Society
Marsha Davis
211 Sequiah Wy, Kalispell, MT 59901
406/752-3319

Nevada Watercolor Society
Susan Fridley
PO Box 27224, Las Vegas, NV 89134
702/255-3490
Sponsors competitive exhibitions, holds classes and seminars, has an art library and publishes a newsletter edited by Mary Hill.

Essex WaterColor Club
Mary Bobeck
41 Ellers Dr, Chatham, NJ 07928

Northeast Watercolor Society
Joan Ross
Box 94, RR 3, Highland Lakes, NJ 07422

New Jersey Watercolor Society
Pat Denman
3430 Hwy 66, Neptune, NJ 07753
201/922-9127

Garden State Watercolor Society
Martha McKinnon
91 Edgestowne Rd, Princeton, NJ 08540

New Mexico Watercolor Society
M Culpepper
PO Box 26884, Albuquerque, NM 87125

Brooklyn Watercolor Society
Charles Gerhart
52 Clark St #8E, Brooklyn, NY 11201
718/624-7660 ext 7805
Sponsors competitive exhibitions, gives scholarships, sponsors classes and has a slide registry.

Niagara Frontier Watercolor Society
Lorna Berlin
59 Catherine St, Buffalo, NY 14221
716/663-9450
Sponsors a national exhibition, classes and seminars, has a video library, a slide registry of shows and a newsletter "Waterbucket," edited by D Meyer.

Cazenovia Watercolor Society
Sue Johnson
8933 Syracuse Rd, Cazenovia , NY 13035

Aquarelle Club
Beverly Schmitt
41 Highfield Rd, Glen Cove, NY 11542

Upper Hudson Watercolor Society
Bill Brender
121 Maple St, Glens Falls, NY 12801

Central NY Watercolor Society
Gretchen Nass
6895 Driftwood Dr, Liverpool, NY 13088

American Watercolor Society
Margery Soroka
47 Fifth Ave, New York, NY 10003
212/206-8986

North East Watercolor Society
Frieda Strobl
50 Old Mtn Rd, Port Jervis, NY 12771

Orange County Watercolor Society
Mary Endico
PO Box 31, Sugar Loaf, NY 10981

Hudson River Watercolor
PO Box 44, Tillson, NY 12486-0044

Watercolor Society of North Carolina
Alice McCallum
6010 Sharon Rd, Charlotte, NC 28210

Northern Kentucky Watercolor Society
Ruthanne Logan
8880 Livingston Rd, Cincinnati, OH 45247

Western Ohio Watercolor Society
Elaine Szelestey
418 E Salem St, Clayton, OH 45315

Central Ohio Watercolor Society
Pamela Graham
141 Ann Ct, Lancaster, OH 43130

Ohio Watercolor Society
Donna Noice
1377 Graf St, Lancaster, OH 43130

Northwestern Ohio Watercolor Society
Lester Cowell
2426 Ross St, Northwood, OH 43619

Mahoning Valley Watercolor Society
Suzanne Anzellotti
2453 Ridgeview Ln Youngstown, OH 44514

Oklahoma Watercolor Society
George Murry
2936 Alexander Ln, Bethany, OK 73008

Oklahoma Watercolor Association
BJ White
13 Pleasant Oak, Edmond, OK 73034

Watercolor Society of Oregon
Ray Zandonotti
11680 SW Denfield, Beaverton, OR 97005

Northwest Watercolor Society
Donna Watson
19775 SW Taposa Pl, Tualatin, OR 97062

Philadelphia Watercolor Club
Ann Howes
383 Hillside Rd, King of Prussia, PA 19406

Pennsylvania Watercolor Society
Ann Fitzpatrick
PO Box 626, Mechanicsburg, PA 17055
Newsletter.

Pittsburgh Watercolor Society
JA Eiser
6300 Fifth Ave, Pittsburgh, PA 15232
412/362-0873
Has a gallery space, competitive exhibitions and a newsletter "Aqueous Medium," edited by Margarette Walk.

Rhode Island Watercolor Society
Kathy Bierwas
Slater Mem Park, Armistice Blvd, Pawtucket, RI 02861
401/726-1876

Tennessee Watercolor Society
Barbara Champlin
2374 Ridgeland, Memphis, TN 38119

Waterloo Watercolor Society
Jane Moseley
1430 Yaupon Valley Rd, Austin, TX 78746

Western Federation of Watercolor Society
Debby Shannon
6515 Northport Dr, Dallas, TX 75230

Society of Watercolor Artists
Judy Sager
320 N Bailey Ave, Ft Worth, TX 76107

Watercolor Art Society
George Bloxsom
1601 W Alabama, Houston, TX 77006
713/942-9966
"Washrag."

Arlington Society of Watercolor Artists
Irene Davis
34 Caddo Pk, Joshua, TX 76058

West Texas Watercolor Society
Box 6621, Lubbock, TX 79493-6621

San Antonio Watercolor Group
Robert Johnson
505 Harrison Ave, San Antonio, TX 78209

Texas Watercolor Society
Marilu Reiffert
723 Clearview, San Antonio, TX 78228

Utah Watercolor Society
Marilyn Thomas
1654 Millbrook Rd, Salt Lake City, UT 84106

Washington Water Color Association
Ina Schecter
7306 Stafford Rd, Alexandria, VA 22307

Shenandoah Valley Watercolor Society
Mary Ann Baugher
412 Park Ave, Elkton, VA 22827

Chesapeake Bay Watercolorists
Jan Vermilya
521 N Claypool Ct, Virginia Beach, VA 23464

Organizations

Watercolor Organizations (cont.)

Northwest Watercolor Society
Helen Oakland
10700 NE Torvanger Rd, Bainbridge Island, WA 98110
206/842-0168
Sponsors competitive exhibitions, gives financial aid to student artists (grants), sponsors workshops, has a slide reigstry, has a video library and publishes "Hot Press Newsletter," edited by Clifford Burkey.

Eastern Washington Watercolor Society
Jeanne Burnham
PO Box 1701, Richland, WA 99352
509/627-0105
Newsletter.

Spokane Watercolor Society
Eleanor Marcus
2212 S Blake Rd, Spokane, WA 99216
206/926-8820

Southwest Washington Watercolor Society
Lucille Hulburt
5515 NE 58th St, Vancouver, WA 98661

West Virginia Watercolor Society
Dava Dahlgran
32 Suzanne St, Rt 1, Washington, WV 26181

Ohio Watercolor Society
Marilyn Phillis
72 Stamm Cir, Wheeling, WV 26003

Madison Watercolor Society
Edward Mayland
5117 Whitcomb Dr, Madison, WI 53711

Wisconsin Watercolor Society
Gene Souders
3462 N 95th St, Milwaukee, WI 53222

Scotch and Watercolor Society
Jean Goedicke
2125 S Coffman, Casper, WY 82604

Use these listings to network, especially in your local areas, but also in other less familiar areas of the country. Listed alphabetically by state, then city within the state.

❖ Selma and Dallas County Council on the Arts
Andry Wood
816 Selma Ave, Selma, AL 36701
334/874-2177 334/874-1210 Fax

Arts council
Grants
Residencies
Newsletter

❖ Galeria Mesa
Robert Schultz
PO Box 1466, 155 N Center St, Mesa, AZ 85211-1466
602/644-2056 602/644-2901 Fax

Public art organization
Gallery
Competitions
Grants   Scholarships   Residencies
Newsletter: *Galeria Review*
Classes/seminars

❖ Southwestern Artist Association
Don Levenson
PO Box 483, Prescott, AZ 86302
520/778-1990 Telephone/Fax

Private organization
Competitions
Newsletter: *Reflections*/Don Preiss, Editor

❖ Sedona Arts Center
Charles Raison
PO Box 569, Sedona, AZ 86339-0569
520/282-3809 Telephone/Fax

Private organization
Gallery
Competitions
Newsletter
Classes/seminars

❖ Tubac Center for the Arts
Judy Eakin
PO Box 1911, Tubac, AZ 85646
520/398-2371

Public art organization
Gallery
Competitions
Classes/seminars
Art library

❖ THEARTFOUNDATION
Lorraine Benini
520 Central Ave, Hot Springs, AR 71901
501/623-9847 501/623-0474
501/623-9847 Fax

Private company
Art library

❖ Crawford County Art Association
Mary Smith
104 N 13th St, Van Buren, AR 72956
501/474-7767

Public art organization
Gallery
Competitions
Newsletter: *Area Art News*/Mildred Peak, Editor
Classes/seminars
Gift shop as well as art supply sales

❖ Gallery of the Center for Psychological Studies
Margaret Alati
1398 Solano Ave, Albany, CA 94706
510/524-0291 510/653-6231 Fax

Private organization
Gallery. We have receptions, publicity, but no cash cahnges ahnds—barter only.
Competitions
Classes and seminars for art therapists

❖ Berkeley Civic Arts Program
Angela Johnson
2180 Milvia St 5Fl, Berkeley, CA 94704
510/644-6309 510/644-6035 Fax

Arts council
Gallery
Newsletter: *Arts & Culture*

❖ Fairfield Civic Arts
Civic Arts Manager
1000 Webster St, Fairfield, CA 94533
707/428-7662 707/428-7628 Fax

Public art organization
Gallery
Classes/seminars
Art library

Organizations

❖ Gualala Arts Inc
Karel Metcalf
PO Box 244, 38001 Old Stage Rd, Gualala,
CA 95445
707/884-1138 Telephone/Fax

Public art organization
Gallery
Competitions
Financial aid to local high school graduates
Newsletter: *Sketches*/Dorothy Rugf, Editor
Classes/seminars
Art library

❖ Freedomist Art Center & Exhibition Space/ FACES
Mr Saúl
528 E Broadway, Long Beach, CA 90802
310/432-3578

Private company
Gallery
Competitions
Residencies
Store with art goods
Classes/seminars in sculpture, ceramics and
pottery

❖ Long Beach Arts
Mel Finley
447 Long Beach Blvd, PO Box 948,
Long Beach, CA 90801
310/435-5995

Private organization
Gallery
Competitions
Newsletter
Classes/seminars
Slide registry

❖ LACE
Matt Easton
6522 Hollywood Blvd, Los Angeles, CA
90028
213/957-1777 213/957-9025 Fax

Private organization
Gallery
Competitions

❖ Alpine County Arts Commission
Kelly Green
PO Box 546, 3 Webster St, Markleeville, CA
96120
916/694-ARTS 916/694-2478 Fax

Arts council
Gallery
Competitions
Residencies
Classes/seminars

❖ Artist's Alliance of California
Bonnie Hall
PO Box 2424, Nevada City, CA 95959
916/272-7357 Telephone/Fax

Private organization
Newsletter: *Review*/Katie Harrison, Editor
*We provide discounts on products and services as
well as a vehicle for the artist to network and
expose his/her work. Organizes inexpensive re-
treats in Europe.*

❖ Center for the Visual Arts/CVA
C Tomye Neal-Madison
713 Washington St, Oakland, CA 94607
510/451-6300 510/763-9970 Fax

Public art organization
Gallery
Competitions
Classes
Slide registry with over 40,000 slides

❖ Pacific Grove Art Center
Joanna Chapman
PO Box 633, 568 Lighthouse Ave,
Pacific Grove, CA 93950
408/375-2208

Non-profit organization
Gallery/Connie Pearlstein
*We are seeking both new and established talent.
We review artwork at three-month intervals. We
do not carry an artist's work permanently.*

❖ Quilt San Diego
Thayes Hower
9747 Business Park Ave #228, San Diego, CA
92131
916/695-2822

Private organization
Competitions
Classes/seminars

Organizations

❖ **Artist Council of the Palm Springs Desert Museum**
Carole Hicks
PO Box 2288, Palm Springs, CA 92263
619/324-7186

Arts council
Bookstore
Classes/seminars

❖ **Japantown Art & Media Workshop**
Dennis Taniguchi
1840 Sutter St #102, San Francisco, CA 94115
415/922-8700 415/922-8700 Fax

Public art organization
Competitions
Newsletter: *Jam*/Mun Yee Tse, Editor
Classes/seminars

❖ **The Lab**
Laura Brun
1807 Divisadero St, San Francisco, CA 94115
415/346-4063

Public art organization
Gallery
Residencies
Classes/seminars

❖ **Orange County Center for Contemporary Art**
Jeffrey Frisch
3621 W MacArthur Blvd #111, Santa Ana, CA 92704
714/549-4989

Private organization
Gallery
Competitions
Newsletter: *ArtSpeak*/Dean Gerrie, Editor
Bookstore (by late 1996)

❖ **Santa Barbara Contemporary Arts Forum**
Nancy Doll
653 Paseo Nuevo, Santa Barbara, CA 93101
805/966-5373 805/962-1421 Fax

Private organization
Gallery
Competitions
Honoraria
Newsletter: *Forum*/Nancy Doll, Editor
Bookstore/Carolyn Bush
Classes/seminars
Art library

❖ **Stockton Arts Commission**
Vince Perrin
Stockton City Hall, 425 N El Dorado St, Stockton, CA 95202
209/937-7488 209/937-7149 Fax

Arts council
Gallery
Competitions
Scholarships
Newsletter: *City Scape*
Classes/seminars
Art library

❖ **Stanford Art Spaces**
Priscilla Hexter
Center for Integrated Systems, Stanford U, Stanford, CA 94305-4070
415/725-3622 415/725-6278 Fax

University organization
Gallery
Newsletter
Bookstore
Classes/seminars
Art library

❖ **Northeast Valley Arts Council**
L Musgrave
13000 Sayre St, Sylmar, CA 91342
818/362-3220 818/364-7755 Fax

Arts council
Century Gallery
Competitions
Classes/seminars

❖ **Sierra Artists' Network**
Betty Corison
PO Box 6354, 380 N Lake Blvd, Tahoe City, CA 96145
916/581-2787

Private organization
Gallery
Competitions
Newsletter/Ellen McBride, Editor
Classes/seminars

Organizations

❖ Vacaville Art League and Gallery
Margie Vasconcelos
718 E Monte Vista Ave, Vacaville, CA 95688
707/448-8712

Public art organization
Gallery
Competitions
Newsletter
Bookstore
Classes/seminars
Art library

❖ Valley Center Art Association
Maryann Miller
29809 Anthony Rd, Valley Center, CA 92082
619/749-9124

Private organization
Gallery
Competitions
Newsletter: *Art-I-Facts*/Ed Miles, Editor

❖ Sparc Gallery
Barbara Jones
685 Venice Blvd, Venice, CA 90291
310/822-9560 310/827-8717 Fax

Social and public art resource center

❖ Mendocino County Arts Council
Rhoda Teplow
400 E Commercial St, Willits, CA 95490
707/937-5611 Telephone/Fax

Arts council/Public art organization
Gallery
Competitions
Grants
Newsletter: *MCAC Newsletter*
Bookstore/Bobbie Yokum

❖ Fremont Center for the Arts
Monica Hinson
505 Macon Ave, PO Box 1006, Canon City,
CO 81215-1006
303/275-2790

Arts council
Gallery
Competitions
Newsletter: *Artifacts*
Gift store
Classes/seminars

❖ Durango Arts Center
Barbara Conrad
835 Main St #210, Durango, CO 81301
970/259-2606 970/259-6570 Fax

Arts council
Gallery
Competitions
Newsletter
Bookstore/Mary Pullar
Slide registry
Art library

❖ One West Art Center
Angela Brayham
201 S College, Ft Collins, CO 80524
970/482-2787

Private organization
Gallery
Competitions
Newsletter
Classes/seminars
Slide registry
Art library

❖ Ouray County Arts Association
Patricia Wilson
PO Box 217, 295 N Lena, Ridgway, CO
81432
970/626-5452

Arts council
Competitions
Scholarships
Classes/seminars

❖ O'Connor Workshops
Harold O'Connor
PO Box 416, 432 H St, Salida, CO 81201
719/539-7519

Private organization
Residencies
Classes/seminars

❖ Brookfield Craft Center
John Russell
PO Box 122, Rte 25, Brookfield, CT 06804
203/775-4526 203/740-7815 Fax

Non-profit organization
Gallery
Competitions
Newsletter: *Brookfield Quarterly*
Bookstore
Classes/seminars

❖ Greenwich Arts Council
Patricia McDonald
299 Greenwich Ave, Greenwich, CT 06830
203/622-3998   203/622-3980 Fax

Private organization/Arts council
Gallery
Competitions
Newsletter
Seminars

❖ Kent Art Association
Constance Horton
21 S Main St, PO Box 202, Kent, CT 06757
203/927-3989

Public art organization
Competitions

❖ Arts & Crafts Association of Meridien Inc
Lillian Carney
53 Colony St, PO Box 348, Meridien, CT 06450
203/235-5347

Public art organization
Gallery
Competitions
Newsletter
Classes/seminars
Art library

❖ Middletown Commission on the Arts
Corinne Gill
PO Box 1300, 245 DeKoven Dr, Middletown, CT 06457
203/344-1491   203/344-0136 Fax

Public art organization
Competitions
Grants
Classes/seminars
Art library

❖ Academic Artists Association
Fran Scully
170 East St S, Suffield, CT 06078
203/668-2787

Public art organization
Competitions

❖ Westport Arts Center
Marilyn Hersey
17 Morningside Dr S, Westport, CT 06880
203/226-1806   203/222-0036 Fax

Arts council
Gallery
Competitions
Newsletter: *Fanfare*/Colleen Grant, Editor
Classes/seminars
Slide registry

❖ Cultural Alliance of Greater Washington
Jennifer Cover Payne
410 8th St NW #600, Washington, DC 20004
202/638-2406   202/638-3388 Fax

Private organization
Newsletter: *Arts Washington*/Jennifer Koedersheimer, Editor

❖ National Artists Equity Association Inc
Linda Church
PO Box 28068, Central Station, Washington, DC 20038
202/628-9633

Private organization
Newsletter: *Pen, Pencil & Paint Arts Advocate*/Joy Turnea Luke & Suzanne Grinnan, Editors
Seminars
Health insurance
Professional services

❖ Manatee County Cultural Alliance
Eileen Hoffner
4301 32nd St W #E-23, Bradenton, FL 34221
813/758-0058   813/753-1482 Fax

Arts council
Competitions
Newsletter

❖ Cultural Affairs
Mary Becht
100 S Andrews Ave, Ft Lauderdale, FL 33301
305/357-7457   305/357-5769 Fax

Arts council
Gallery
Grants to cultural organizations
Magazine: *Cultural Quarterly*/Jody Horne-Leshinsky, Editor
Seminars
Slide registry

Organizations

❖ National Association of Fine Artists/NAFA
PO Box 4189, Ft Lauderdale, FL 33388
800/996-NAFA

Private organization
Newsletter
Offer discounts on art supplies, insurance, auto rental, long distance calls and more.

❖ Lee County Alliance of the Arts
Gladys Land
10091 McGregor Blvd, Ft Myers, FL 33919
813/939-2787 813/939-0794 Fax

Public art organization
Gallery
Competitions
Newsletter: *Kaleidoscope*/Shann Holiday, Editor
Bookstore
Classes/seminars
Art library

❖ Thomas Center Galleries
Ann Baird
DCNO, Box 490/Station 30, Gainesville, FL 32602
904/334-2197 904/334-2314 Fax

Public art organization
Gallery
Seminars

❖ Pasco Fine Arts Council
Suzan Kroul
5477 Moog Rd, Holiday, FL 34690-2354
813/845-7322

Arts council
Gallery
Newsletter: *PFAC Newsletter*
Classes on painting, sculpture, calligraphy, drama and singing
Art library

❖ Artists Showplace Coop Inc
Ruth Klebins
7665 W Lake Worth Rd, Lake Worth, FL 33467
407/966-4908

Public art organization/cooperative
Gallery
Competitions
Newsletter/Schedule of Events
Classes/seminars

❖ Brevard Art Center & Museum
Randall Hayes
1463 Highland Ave, PO Box 360835,
Melbourne, FL 32936
407/242-0737

Private organization
Gallery
Competitions
Newsletter
Bookstore
Classes/seminars
Art library

❖ Naples Art Association
Anne Bennett
970 5th Ave N, Naples, FL 33940
813/262-6517 Telephone/Fax

Public art organization
Gallery
Competitions
Scholarships
Newsletter
Bookstore
Classes/seminars
Art library

❖ Florida Division of Cultural Affairs, Dept of State
Peyton Fearington
2475 Apalachee Pkwy, Tallahassee, FL 32301
904/487-2980 904/922-5259 Fax

Arts council
Gallery
Fellowships
Newsletter: *Informational Memo* /Kathy Engerran, Editor

❖ Artists Unlimited Inc
Genie Farrell White
223 N 12th St, The Channel District, Tampa, FL 33602
813/229-5958

Public art organization
Gallery
Competitions
Newsletter
Bookstore
Classes/seminars
Slide registry
Art library

Organizations

❖ **Georgia Artists Registry**
Atlanta College of Art
1280 Peachtree St NE, Atlanta, GA 30309
404/898-1164

❖ **Southern Arts Federation**
Jeffrey Kesper
181 14th St NE #400, Atlanta, GA 30309
404/874-7244 404/873-2148 Fax

Arts council
Fellowships/Residencies
Newsletter

❖ **Golden Isles Arts & Humanities Association**
Helen Alexander
1530 Newcastle St, Brunswick, GA 31520
912/262-6934 912/262-1029 Fax

Arts council
Gallery
Competitions
Newsletter: *Spotlight*

❖ **South Cobb Arts Alliance**
Kathy Heimann
5239 Floyd Rd, Mableton, GA 30059
404/739-0189

Public art organization
Gallery
Competitions
Newsletter: *NewsNotes*/Susan Gardner, Editor
Classes
Art library

❖ **The Glynn Art Association**
Kay Wayne
319 Mallory St, PO Box 20673,
St Simons Island, GA 31522
912/638-8770 912/634-8506 Fax

Public art organization
Gallery
Competitions
Scholarships to at-risk children
Newsletter: *GAA Quarterly*
Classes/seminars

❖ **Ohoopee Regional Council for the Arts**
Mary Lea Lane
PO Box 1241, 117 SE Main St, Vidalia, GA 30474
912/537-8459 912/538-7766 Fax

Arts council
Gallery
Newsletter: *Orca Matters*
Classes

❖ **Volcano Art Center**
Marilyn Nicholson
PO Box 104, Hawaii National Park, HI 96718
808/967-8222 808/967-8512 Fax

Private organization
Gallery
Newsletter: *Volcano Gazette*/Ter DePuy, Editor
Classes

❖ **Queen Emma Gallery**
Masa Morioka Taira
PO Box 861, Honolulu, HI 96808
808/547-4397 808/547-4646 Fax

Private organization
Gallery

❖ **Idaho Commission on the Arts**
Margot Knight
PO Box 83720, Boise, ID 83720-0008
208/334-2119 208/334-2488 Fax

State art organization
Fellowships   Grants
Newsletter: *Latitudes*/Diane Josephy Pearney, Editor
Seminars & workshops

❖ **Aurora Public Art Commission**
Peggy Moses
44 E Downer Pl, Aurora, IL 60507-2067
708/844-3640 708/892-0741 Fax

Public art organization
Gallery/construction underway for Fall 1995
Competitions
Scholarships   Residencies
Classes
Art library

Organizations

❖ Contemporary Art Workshop
Lynn Kearney
542 W Grant Pl, Chicago, IL 60614
312/472-4004

Nonprofit organization
Gallery/showcasing primarily young emerging
artists from mid-west region
Classes
Slide registry of artists who have shown

❖ ETA Creative Arts Foundation Inc
Abena Joan Brown
7558 S Chicago Ave, Chicago, IL 60619
312/752-3955 312/752-8727 Fax

Nonprofit organization
Gallery
Concession stand
Theater library

❖ Greenview Arts Center
Nicholas De Wolff
6418 N Greenview, Chicago, IL 60626
312/508-0085 312/508-9400 Fax

Private organization
Gallery
Newsletter: *Viewpoint*

❖ Illinois Art Gallery
Kent Smith
100 W Randolph #20-200, Chicago, IL 60601
312/814-5322

Public art organization
Gallery
Newsletter for membership only
Classes/seminars

❖ Near Northwest Arts Council
Laura Weatherfed
1579 N Milwaukee Ave, Chicago, IL 60622
312/278-7677 312/278-8451 Fax

Arts council
Gallery
Competitions
Residencies
Newsletter: *Context*
Classes/seminars
Slide registry
Art library

❖ Textile Arts Center
Gina Alicea
916 W Diversey, Chicago, IL 60614
312/929-5655 312/929-9837 Fax

Public art organization
Gallery
Competitions
Newsletter: *TAC Newsletter*
Classes
Slide registry
Art library

❖ Northwest Area Arts Council
Mary Obodzinski
100 W Municipal Complex, Crystal lake, IL
60014
815/459-2020 ext 334 815/459-2350 Fax

Arts council
Competitions
Scholarships
Newsletter: *Artbeat*/Tina Nystrom, Editor
Seminars

❖ Art Encounter
Joanna Prinsky
927 Noyes St, Evanston, IL 60201
708/328-9222

Nonprofit organization
Calendar of Events/Spring and Fall
Classes/seminars/gallery walks, tours and trips
around the country

❖ Park Forest Art Center
PO Box 776, 410 Lakewood Blvd,
Park Forest, IL 60466
708/748-3377

Nonprofit organization
Gallery
Competitions
Newsletter
Classes/seminars

❖ Columbus Area Arts Council
Lewis Bieri
302 Washington St, Columbus, IN 47201
812/376-2539 812/376-2589 Fax

Arts council
Gallery (fee for private use)
Newsletter: *Quarterly Review*

❖ **Indiana Arts Commission**
Dorothy Ilgen
402 W Washington #072, Indianapolis, IN
46204
317/232-1268 317/232-5595 Fax

Arts council
Gallery
Fellowships   Residencies

❖ **Jay County Arts Council**
Eric Rogers
138 E Main, PO Box 804, Portland, IN 47371
219/726-4809

Arts council
Gallery
Competitions
Residencies
Newsletter: *The Main Artery*
Classes

❖ **Iowa City/Johnson County Arts Council**
Anne Gochenour
129 E Washington LL, Jefferson Bldg,
Iowa City, IA 52240
319/337-7447

Arts council
Gallery
Competitions
Newsletter: *Art Sheet*/JoAnn Castagna, Editor
Classes/seminars
Art library

❖ **Coffeyville Cultural Arts Council Inc**
Kenneth Burchinal
PO Box 487, 912 Walnut, Coffeyville, KS
67337-0487
316/251-0088

Arts council
Gallery
Newsletter: *State of the Arts*/Judy Hill, Editor
Bookstore
Classes

❖ **Fredonia Arts Council Inc**
Cassandra Edson
PO Box 355, 320 N 7th St, Fredonia, KS
66736
316/378-2052

Arts council
Gallery
Classes

❖ **Carnegie Arts Center Inc**
R Johnson & ME Maxwell
PO Box 501, 601 S Fifth St, Leavenworth, KS
66048
913/651-0765 913/682-2248 Fax

Private organization
Gallery
Classes/seminars

❖ **Society of Decorative Painters**
414 N Main #200, PO Box 808, Newton, KS
67114
316/283-9665 316/283-5048 Fax

Public art organization
Competitions
Newsletter: *Decorative Painter*/Julie Vosberg,
Editor
Classes/seminars
Art library

❖ **Salina Art Center**
Saralyn Reece Hardy
PO Box 743, 242 S Santa Fe, Salina, KS
67402
913/827-1431 Telephone/Fax

Private organization
Gallery
Competitions
Residencies
Newsletter
Classes/seminars
Art library

❖ **Wichita Center for the Arts**
Jerry Jensen
9112 E Central, Wichita, KS 67208
316/634-ARTS 316/634-0593 Fax

Private organization
Gallery
Competitions
Scholarships
Newsletter: *Center News*/Cindy Carpenter,
Editor
Classes/seminars
Art library

Organizations

❖ **Lexington Art League**
Jerry McGee
209 Castlewood Dr, Lexington, KY 40505
703/687-6701 703/687-6701 Fax

Public art organization
Gallery
Competitions
Scholarships
Newsletter: *Mixed Media*/Clair Talmadge,
Editor
Classes/seminars
Slide registry
Art library

❖ **Louisville Visual Art Association**
John Begley
3005 River Rd, Louisville, KY 40207
502/896-2146 502/896-2148 Fax

Private organization
Gallery
Competitions
Newsletter: *Visual Arts Review*/Richard Boling,
Editor
Classes/seminars
Slide registry

❖ **Baton Rouge Gallery**
Kathleen Sunderman
1442 City Park Ave, Baton Rouge, LA 70808
504/383-1470 504/336-0943 Fax

Public art organization
Gallery
Newsletter: *In Touch*/Larry Giacoletti, Editor

❖ **Contemporary Arts Center**
Ted Potter
PO Box 30498, New Orleans, LA 70190
504/523-1216 504/528-3828 Fax

Public art organization
Gallery
Competitions
Newsletter
Bookstore (by 1996-97)

❖ **Slidell Cultural Center**
Suzanne Parsons
PO Box 828, Slidell, LA 70459
504/646-4375 504/646-4231 Fax

Public art organization
Gallery
Competitions
Grants
Newsletter: *Bravo!*/Merna Bridgeman, Editor
Classes/seminars
Slide registry
Art library
Produce a 30-minute TV Show on Cable,
"Access on the Arts"

❖ **Round Top Center for the Arts**
Nancy Freeman
PO Box 1316, Bus Rte 1, Damariscotta, ME
04543
207/563-1507

Nonprofit arts institution
Gallery
Scholarships to youth
Bookstore/Connie Pace
Classes/seminars
Art library

❖ **Cultural Arts Foundation of Anne Arundel
County Inc**
Carol Treiber
2664 Riva Rd #6304, Annapolis, MD 21401
410/222-7949 410/222-7255 Fax

Arts council
Gallery
Newsletter: *Arts Almanac*/Carol Denny, Editor

❖ **Maryland Hall for the Creative Arts**
Michael Bailey
801 Chase St, Annapolis, MD 21401
410/263-5544 410/263-5114 Fax

Private organization
Gallery
Competitions
Newsletter: *Art-a-Facts*/Theresa Strobel, Editor
Classes
Art library

❖ Howard County Art Guild
Gina Somerlock
3681 Sharp Rd, Glenwood, MD 21738
410/442-1298

Private organization
Gallery
Competitions
Scholarships
Newsletter: *News & Views*
Classes/seminars
Slide registry
Art library

❖ International Council for Cultural Exchange/ ICCE
Stanley Gochman
1559 Rockville Pike, Rockville, MD 20852
301/983-9479

Non-profit cultural educational organization, sponsors classes in painting in Europe

❖ U of Mass Arts Council
Marlene Housner
103 Hasbrouck Hall, Amherst, MA 01003
413/545-0202

Arts council/Public art organization
Gallery—several on campus
Competitions
Grants
Newsletter: *ArtSitings*
Classes/seminars

❖ Art Institute of Boston
Stan Trecker
700 Beacon St, Boston, MA 02215
617/262-1223 617/437-1226 Fax

Private organization
Gallery
Fellowships: *$15,000 DuPont Fellowship for minority photographic artists/April 1 deadline/ call for prospectus.*
Classes

❖ Photographic Resource Center at Boston U
John Jacob
602 Commonwealth Ave, Boston, MA 02215
617/353-0700 617/353-1662 Fax

Public art organization
Gallery
Competitions
Newsletter: *PRC & Views*
Classes/seminars
Slide registry
Art library

❖ Society of Arts & Crafts
Bethe Ann Gerstein
175 Newbury St, Boston, MA 02116
617/266-1810 617/266-5654 Fax

Private organization
Gallery
Newsletter/Leith Farragher, Editor
Seminars
Slide registry

❖ South Shore Art Center
Lanci Valentine
119 Ripley Rd, Cohasset, MA 02025
617/383-ARTS (2787) Telephone/Fax

Private organization
Gallery
Competitions
Scholarships
Newsletter: *Artline*/Rhonda Myers, Editor
Classes/seminars
Slide registry
Art library

❖ Arts Council of Franklin County
Paula Gottlieb
PO Box 364, 7 Franklin St, Greenfield, MA 01302
413/772-6811

Arts council
Gallery/*Artspace*
Newsletter
Classes/seminars
Slide registry

❖ Art & Soul
Barbara Cunha
PO Box 97, 10 Elm St, Massonet, MA 02702
508/644-2433

Private organization
Classes/seminars
Slide registry

❖ The New Art Center
61 Washington Park, Box 330, Newtonville, MA 02160
617/964-3424

Private organization
Gallery
Classes/seminars

Organizations

❖ Contemporary Artists Center
Eric Rudd
189 Beaver St, North Adams, MA 01247
413/663-9555 413/664-4549 Fax

Private organization
Gallery
Competitions
Scholarships
Classes/seminars

❖ Berkshire Artisans
Daniel O'Connell
28 Renne Ave, Pittsfield, MA 01201
413/499-9348

Public art organization
Gallery
Classes
Slide registry

❖ Open Art Studios in Sudbury/OASIS
Janice Corkin Rudolf
37 Atkinson Ln, Sudbury, MA 01776
508/443-5104

Private organization
Gallery
Competitions
Classes/seminars
Slide registry

❖ Michigan Guild of Artists & Artisans
Mary Strope
118 N Fourth Ave, Ann Arbor, MI 48104
313/662-3382 313/662-0339 Fax

Private organization
Gallery
Newsletter: *Limited Edition*/Sara Wheeler,
Editor
Seminars
Slide registry

❖ Detroit Focus
Carlene Carroll
33 E Grand River, Detroit, MI
313/965-3245

Public art organization
Gallery
Competitions
Newsletter/Vince Carducci, Editor
Classes/seminars

❖ Farrington Keith Creative Art Center
Susannah Keith
8099 Main St, Dexter, MI 48130
313/426-0236

Private organization
Gallery
Competitions

❖ Urban Institute for Contemporary Arts
Marjorie Kuipers
88 Monroe SE, Grand Rapids, MI 49503
616/454-7000 616/454-7013 Fax

Private organization
Gallery
Newsletter: *UICA Newsletter*

❖ Copper Country Community Arts Council
Cynthia Cote
126 Quincy St, Hancock, MI 49930
906/482-2333

Arts council
Gallery
Competitions
Newsletter: *CCCAC News*/Karen Bell-Hanson,
Editor
Classes/seminars
Art library

❖ Arts Council of Greater Kalamazoo
CJ Grantham
201 W Kalamazoo, Kalamazoo, MI 49007
616/342-5059 616/342-6531 Fax

Arts council
Gallery
Competitions
Grants   Scholarships
Newsletter: *Metropolitan Artlines*

❖ Downriver Council for the Arts
Angela Petroff
2630 Biddle Ave, Wyandotte, MI 48192
313/281-2787 313/281-0709 Fax

Arts council
Competitions
Newsletter: *Arts and . . .*/Judy Gullan, Editor
Classes/seminars

❖ **Bemidji Community Arts Center**
Diane Field
426 Bemidji Ave, Bemidji, MN 56601
218/751-7570

Arts council
Gallery
Competitions
Newsletter: *Newsletter*/Rebecca Windschitl,
Editor
Bookstore
Classes
Slide registry
Art library

❖ **Elk River Area Arts Council**
David Beauvais
400 Jackson Ave #205, Elk River, MN 55330
612/441-4725

Arts council
Gallery
Competitions
Newsletter: *Eddy*
Seminars

❖ **Mankato Area Arts Council**
Carnegie Arts Center
120 S Broad St, Mankato, MN 56001
507/625-2730

Private organization/Arts council
Gallery
Bookstore/Fine art books and regional artwork
Classes
Slide registry of past exhibitions
Art library in process

❖ **Southwest Minnesota Arts & Humanities Council**
Robert Ross
PO Box 1193, Marshall, MN 56258
507/537-1471 Telephone/Fax

Arts council/Public art organization
Competitions
Grants/Residencies
Newsletter: *Voices*
Classes/seminars

❖ **Below the Surface Printmakers Atelier**
Denese Sanders
27 N Fourth St #301, Minneapolis, MN
55401
612/340-1001

Private organization
Gallery space for exhibition once a year
Classes/seminars
Slide registry
Provides printmaking facilities (etching,
monotype, woodcut) to artists of all back-
grounds. Access is obtained on a monthly basis
with varying prices depending on length of
contract.

❖ **Split Rock Arts Program**
University of MN/Andrea Gilats
306 Wesbrook Hall, 77 Pleasant St SE,
Minneapolis, MN 55455
612/624-6800 612/625-2568 Fax

Higher education institute
Scholarships
Classes

❖ **Minnesota State Arts Board**
Sam Grabarski
432 Summit Ave, St Paul, MN 55102-2624
612/297-2603 612/297-4304 Fax

Arts council
Fellowships   Grants   Residencies
Newsletter: *Art Board News*/Erin Hart, Editor
Slide registry

❖ **Northern Clay Center**
Emily Galusha
2375 University Ave W, St Paul, MN 55114
612/642-1735 612/644-8025 Fax

Private company
Gallery
Competitions
Grants
Newsletter
Store with ceramics
Classes/seminars

❖ **Ocean Springs Art Association**
Judy & Robert MacInnis
PO Box 136, Ocean Springs, MS 39564
601/875-0437

Public art organization
Newsletter
Classes/seminars
Art library

Organizations

❖ ArtCentral
Sandy Higgins
PO Box 189, 308 Central, Carthage, MO
64836
417/358-4404 417/358-2420 Fax

Public art organization
Gallery
Competitions
Scholarships
Newsletter
Classes/seminars
Art library

❖ Art St Louis
Dion Dion
917 Locust St #300, St Louis, MO 63101
314/241-4810 314/241-6933 Fax

Nonprofit organization
Gallery
Competitions
Newsletter: *Art St Louis*/Robin Hirsch
Seminars
Slide registry
Art library

❖ Butte-Silver Bow Arts Foundation
Sharon Knauth
PO Box 622, 321 W Broadway, Butte, MT
59701
406/723-7600 406/723-5083 Fax

Private organization
Competitions
Newsletter: *Chateau Communique*
Classes

❖ Bemis Center for Contemporary Arts
Ree Schonlau
724 S 12th St, Omaha, NE
402/341-7130 402/341-9791 Fax

Private organization
Gallery
Residencies
Art library

❖ Nebraska Arts Council
Jennifer Clark
3838 Davenport, Omaha, NE 68131
402/595-2122 402/595-2334 Fax

State arts council
Fellowships   Residencies
Newsletter: *Flatwater Arts Companion*/Martin
Skomal, Editor

❖ Center for Arts & Spirituality
Norman Cemtois, Elizabeth Rosson, Dorothy
Landry
200 Lowell Rd, Hudson, NH 03051
603/881-9910

Private organization
Gallery
Classes/seminars

❖ AVA Gallery and Art Center
Bente Torjusen
11 Bank St, Lebanon, NH 03766
603/448-3117

Private organization
Gallery for artists from VT and NH
Newsletter
Classes

❖ Morris County Art Association
Dolores Ziegler
10 Catherine Ln, Morristown, NJ
201/267-1722

Public art organization
Competitions
Newsletter
Classes

❖ Institute for Arts & Humanities Education/ IAHE
Jacqueline Rubel
100 Jersey Ave #B-104, New Brunswick, NJ
08901
908/220-1600 908/220-1515 Fax

Nonprofit organization
Residencies
Newsletter: *Newslink & Expression*
Classes/seminars

❖ New Jersey State Council on the Arts
Barbara Russo
CN 306, Trenton, NJ 08625
609/292-6130 609/989-1440 Fax

Arts council/Public art organization
Competitions
Fellowships/In-school residencies
Newsletter: *Report to the Field*/Nina Stack,
Editor
Slide registry

❖ **Woodbridge Township Cultural Arts Commission**
Stephen Kager
582 Rahway Ave, Woodbridge, NJ 07095
908/634-0413

Arts council
Gallery
Competitions
Newsletter
Seminars
Slide registry

❖ **Albuquerque United Artists**
Laurel Wallace
PO Box 1808, Albuquerque, NM 87103
505/243-0531

Nonprofit organization
Competitions
Newsletter/LA Thompson, Editor
Seminars

❖ **New Mexico Potters Association**
Susan Neas
PO Box 26811, Albuquerque, NM 87125
505/246-0742

Private organization
Competitions
Newsletter: *Slip Trails*/Penne Roberts, Editor
Classes/seminars

❖ **Promote Art Works Inc**
Kathleen Laziza
123 Smith St, Brooklyn, NY 11201
718/797-3116

Gallery
Classes for children
Seminars in theater arts

❖ **CEPA Gallery**
Robert Hirsch
700 Main St 4Fl, Buffalo, NY 14202
716/856-2717 716/856-2720 Fax

Private organization
Gallery
Newsletter: *CEPA Journal*/Robert Hirsch, Editor
Bookstore that sells own titles
Classes/seminars
Art library

❖ **Leatherstocking Brush and Palette Club**
Jeanette Koji
PO Box 446, Pioneer Alley, Cooperstown, NY 13326
607/547-8044

Nonprofit organization
Gallery
Scholarships
Newsletter: *Bulletin*/Dorothy Smith, Editor
Classes

❖ **Arts Council of Orange County**
Charles Pickering
19 South St, Middletown, NY 10940
914/342-2133 914/342-1436 Fax

Private organization
Gallery
Competitions
Grants
Classes

❖ **Aesthetic Realism Foundation/Terrain Gallery**
Margot Carpenter
141 Greene St, New York, NY 10012
212/777-4490 212/777-4426 Fax

Nonprofit organization
Gallery
Weekly international periodical: *The Right of Aesthetic Realism to Be Known*/Ellen Reiss, Editor
Bookstore
Classes/seminars
Art library

❖ **Art Initiatives**
Gail Swithenbank
148B Duane St, New York, NY 10013
212/406-4073 212/406-1252 Fax

Private organization
Gallery
Competitions
Newsletter: *Art Initiatives Newsletter*/Peggy Hadden, Editor
Seminars
Slide registry

Organizations

❖ First Street Gallery
Rallou Malliarakis
560 Broadway #402, New York, NY 10012
212/226-9127

Private organization
Gallery

❖ Manhattan Graphics Center
Meredith Mayer
476 Broadway, New York, NY 10013
212/219-8783

Public art organization
Gallery
Classes/seminars/printmaking school and
workshop
Slide registry

❖ New York Foundation for the Arts/NYFA
Ted Berger
155 Ave of the Americas, New York, NY
10013
212/366-6900

Private organization
Fellowships & grants for NY artists only
Newsletter: *FYI*

❖ Phoenix Gallery
Linda Handler
568 Broadway #607, New York, NY 10012
212/226-8711 Telephone/Fax

Artist-run gallery: *Looking for both new and
established talent as new members. Reviews
slides once a month. The gallery provides space
for performances, plays, poetry, music and is
open to the public for a fee of $5.*
Seminars

❖ Port Authority for NY & NJ
SS Wenegrat
1 World Trade Center #820W, New York, NY
10048
212/435-3388 212/435-3382 Fax

Public art organization
Gallery
Competitions
Slide registry

❖ Arts Council for Wyoming County
Joan Effman
1 N Main St, PO Box 249, Perry, NY 14530
716/237-3517

Arts council
Gallery
Grants
Newsletter: *Arts News*/Karen McCulley, Editor

❖ Long Island Arts Council at Freeport
Grace Shen
130 E Merrick Rd, Plainview, NY 11803
516/223-2522 516/223-6991 Fax

Arts council
Competitions
Grants
Newsletter: *Artscene*/Grace Shen, Editor
Classes/seminars
Slide registry

❖ Council on the Arts for Clinton County
Lola Johnson
PO Box 451, 60 Bridge St, Plattsburgh, NY
12901
518/563-5222 518/563-5310 Fax

Arts council
Gallery
Competitions
Grants
Newsletter: *Cultural Connection*/Tarley
Lieberthal, Editor
Workshops

❖ Women's Studio Workshop Inc
Ann Kalmbach
PO Box 489, 722 Binnewater Ln, Rosendale,
NY 12472
914/658-9133 914/658-9031 Fax

Nonprofit organization
Fellowships   Grants
Classes/seminars

❖ Rockland Center for the Arts
Julianne Ramos
27 S Greenbush Rd, West Nyack, NY 10994
914/358-0877 914/358-0971 Fax

Private organization
Gallery
Competitions
Residencies
Newsletter: *ArtLine*
Classes/seminars
Slide registry for Rockland County artists only

Arts Council for the Northern Adirondacks
Caroline Rubino
PO Box 187, 23 N Main St, Westport, NY
12993
518/962-8778 518/962-8797 Fax

Arts council
Gallery/regional artists only
Competitions/regional artists only
Grants/regional artists only
Newsletter: *News & Views*/Susan Hughes,
Editor
Seminars

The Upper Room Gallery
Gayle Tate
28 Hendersonville Rd, Asheville, NC 28803
704/277-7571

Private organization
Gallery
Classes/seminars and weekly meetings to
further the careers of artists
Art library

Cultural Arts Committee of Parks & Recreation
Sarah Sheffield
PO Box 8005, Cary, NC 27512-8005
919/460-4973 919/460-4935 Fax

Public art organization
Gallery
Classes/seminars

North Carolina Nature Artists Association
Carl Regutti
307 Electra Dr, Cary, NC 27513
919/481-2187

Nonprofit organization
Competitions
Newsletter: *NCNAA Newsletter*/Jim Sanders,
Editor
Classes/seminars
Slide registry (notebook of photo pages)

Page-Walker Hotel Arts & History Center
Robbie Stone
PO Box 8005, 119 Ambassador Lp, Cary, NC
27512-8005
919/460-4963

Public art organization
Gallery
Competitions
Classes/seminars

Catawba Valley Visual Arts League
Alyse Berasa
1960 Highway 70 SE, Box 282, Hickory, NC
28603
704/328-8183

Arts council
Gallery
Competitions
Newsletter/L Allen, Editor
Classes/seminars

Community Council for the Arts
Carol Tokarski
PO Box 3554, 400 N Queen St, Kingston, NC
28502
919/527-2517

Arts council
Gallery
Competitions
Grants/Residencies
Newsletter: *Kaleidoscope*
Bookstore
Classes

Craven Arts Council & Gallery
Cary Worthy
PO Box 596, 317 Middle St, New Bern, NC
28563
919/638-2577

Arts council
Gallery
Competitions
Grants
Newsletter: *Luminary*/Susan York, Editor
Classes/seminars

Rocky Mount Arts Center
Marlene Payne
1173 Nashville Rd, PO Box 4031,
Rocky Mount, NC 27803
919/972-1163

Public art organization
Gallery
Competitions
Newsletter: *ArtyFacts*/Britt Vice, Editor
Classes/seminars

Toledo Artists' Club
Toledo Botanical Garden
5403 Elmer Dr, Toledo, OH 43615
419/531-4079

Organizations

❖ Individual Artists of Oklahoma/IAO
Shirley Blaschke
PO Box 60824, Oklahoma City, OK 73146
405/232-6060   405/236-0823 Fax

Private organization
Gallery
Competitions
Newsletter
Classes/seminars
Art library

❖ Corvallis Arts Center/Lin-Benton Council for the Arts
Corby Stonebraker
700 SW Madison Ave, Corvallis, OR 97333
503/754-1551

Private organization/Arts council
Gallery
Competitions
Grants
Newsletter: *Artspirit*/Kim Barker, Editor
Bookstore/Hester Coucke
Classes/seminars
Slide registry

❖ Oregon Coast Council for the Arts
Sharon Morgan
PO Box 1315, 777 W Olive, Newport, OR 97365
503/265-9231   503/265-9464 Fax

Arts council
Gallery
Competitions
Grants   Residencies
Newsletter
Classes/seminars
Slide registry
Art library

❖ Main Line Art Center
Judy Herman
Old Buck Rd & Lancaster Ave, Haverford, PA 19041
610/525-0272   610/525-5036 Fax

Private organization
Gallery
Competitions
Classes/seminars

❖ New Arts Program
James Carroll
173 W Main St, PO Box 82, Kutztown, PA 19530
610/683-6440 Telephone/Fax

Public art organization
Newsletter: *NAP Preview*/John Latte, Editor
Art library, including videos and slides

❖ Community Gallery of Lancaster
Ellen Rosenholtz
135 N Lime St, Lancaster, PA 17602
717/394-3497

Public art organization
Gallery
Newsletter: *Collage*/Ellen Rosenholtz, Editor
Classes/seminars

❖ Manayunk Art Center
Susan Kenney
419 Green Ln (rear), Philadelphia, PA 19128
215/482-3363

Public art organization
Gallery
Competitions/one in spring and one in fall
Newsletter: *Manayunk Art Center Newsletter*/ Elizabeth Tillman, Editor
Classes/seminars
Slide registry
Art library

❖ University City Arts League
Diane Cloutier
4226 Spruce St, Philadelphia, PA 19104
215/382-7811

Private nonprofit organization
Gallery
Classes

❖ Fine Arts Center of Kershaw County
Susan Harper
PO Box 1498, 810 Lyttleton St, Camden, SC 29020
803/425-7676   803/425-7679 Fax

Private organization/Arts council
Competitions
Residencies
Newsletter/S Harder, Editor
Classes/seminars

❖ Upstate Visual Arts
Jayne Jaudon Ferrer
123 W Broad St, Greenville, SC 29601
803/467-3134 803/467-3133 Fax

Public art organization
Gallery
Competitions
Financial aid
Newsletter
Classes/seminars
Slide registry

❖ Hendersonville Arts Council
E Dye
PO Box 64, 252 E Main St, Hendersonville,
TN 37077
615/822-0789

Arts council
Gallery
Classes

❖ Arts Council of Greater Kingsport
Pat Jessee
1200 E Center St, Kingsport, TN 37660
615/392-8421 615/392-8422 Fax

Arts council
Gallery
Competitions
Grants
Newsletter: *The Lively Arts*/Ellen Finney, Editor
Classes/seminars
Art library

❖ Arts Council of Greater Knoxville
Carole Lerch
PO Box 2506, Knoxville, TN 37901
615/523-7543 615/523-7312 Fax

Arts council
Gallery
Competitions
Grants   Residencies
Newsletter: *ArtsPlace*
Classes/seminars
Slide registry
Art library with periodicals.

❖ Dougherty Arts Center
Parks & Maria Cicciarelli
1110 Barton Springs Rd, Austin, TX 78701
512/397-1468 512/397-1451 Fax

Public art organization
Gallery
Competitions
Grants
Cultural Arts Brochure
Classes/seminars
Slide registry (Art in Public Places Office)

❖ Texas Fine Arts Association
Sandra Gregor
3809-B W 35 St, Austin, TX 78703
512/453-5312

Private organization
Gallery
Competitions
Newsletter

❖ Dallas Visual Art Center
Katherine Wagner
2917 Swiss Ave, Dallas, TX 75204
214/821-2522 214/821-9103 Fax

Public art organization
Gallery
Competitions
Newsletter: *Visual Exchange*/Katherine Wagner,
Editor
Classes/seminars
Art resource library

❖ Bridge Center for Contemporary Art
Mary Evelynn Sorrell
127 Pioneer Plz, El Paso, TX 79901
915/532-6707 915/532-6707 Fax

Public art organization
Gallery
Bookstore
Classes/seminars

❖ Odessa Cultural Council
Paul Mastrangelo
PO Box 7195, 205 W University, Odessa, TX
79760
915/337-1492

Arts council
Grants to local artists
Residencies in area schools

Organizations

❖ Barton on Boydstun
Lindy Barton
505 E Boydstun, Rockwall, TX 75087
214/771-4350 214/772-4664 Fax

Private company
Gallery
Newsletter: *Barton on Boydstun*/Edie Barton,
Editor
Classes/seminars
Art library

❖ Vermont Council on the Arts
Nicolette Clarke
136 State St, Drawer 33, Montpelier, VT
05633
802/828-3291

Arts council
Fellowships   Grants
Newsletter: *Artsletter*/Michael Levine, Editor
Slide registry

❖ Western Art Association
Diane Legere
PO Box 893, 416 N Pearl, Ellensburg, WA
98926
509/962-2934

Nonprofit organization
Newsletter: *Brush Strokes*
Sponsors an annual national western art show
and auction for 23 years that features over 200
artists.

❖ Greater Marysville Artist Guild
Debra Teachout-Teashon
PO Box 562, 5833 Parkside Dr, Marysville,
WA 98270
360/653-1914 Telephone/Fax

Public art organization
Competitions
Scholarships
Newsletter: *Artist*
Classes

❖ Mountlake Terrace Arts Commission
Deborah Martin-Bratt
5303 228 SW, Mountlake Terrace, WA
98043
206/776-9173

Municipal arts council
Gallery
Competitions
Classes/seminars

❖ Port Angeles Fine Arts Center
Jake Seniuk
1203 E Lauridsen Blvd, Port Angeles, WA
98362
360/457-3532 360/452-0364 Fax

Public art organization
Gallery
Competitions
Newsletter: *On Center*
Bookstore/Lisa Redlin, buyer

❖ Artist Trust
Marschell Paul
1401 3rd Ave #404, Seattle, WA 98102
206/467-8734 206/467-9633 Fax

Fellowships & grants available/Washington state
residents only
Newsletter: *Artist Trust Journal*/Christina
DePalo, Editor
Seminars

❖ Artsbridge Inc
Lisa Starcher
602 Juliana, PO Box 1706, Parkersburg, WV
26101
304/428-3988 304/428-3989 Fax

Arts council
Grants
Residencies
Newsletter: *Artful*/Mark Weyman, Editor
Classes/seminars
Slide registry
Art library

❖ Appleton Art Center
Jan Hughes
130 N Morrison St, Appleton, WI 54911
414/733-4089

Private non-profit organization
Gallery
Competitions
Newsletter: *Artisan*/Denise Crouse, Editor
Classes

❖ **Wisconsin Painters & Sculptors**
Marilyn Hatfield
1112 Smith St, Green Bay, WI 54302
414/432-8550

Nonprofit juried membership organization
Competitions
Newsletter: *Art in Wisconsin*/Marsha
Tuchscherer, Editor
Classes/seminars open to the general public
Art library

❖ **Dillman's Creative Arts Foundation Inc**
Dennis Robertson
PO Box 98F, 3305 Sand Lake Lodge Ln,
Lac Du Flambeau, WI 54538
715/588-3143 715/588-3110 Fax

Private organization
Gallery
Scholarships
Newsletter: *Creative Workshops Annual*
Bookstore
Classes/seminars
Art library

❖ **Gallery 218**
Walker Point Artists Association
Judith Hooks
218 S 2nd St, Milwaukee, WI 53204
414/277-7800

Cooperative gallery: *Seeking new members*
Gallery
Competitions
Newsletter

❖ **Countryside Artists**
Polly Anderson
134 Fayette St, Phillips, WI 54555
715/339-3465

Nonprofit organization
Gallery
Scholarships for area high school students
Programs/seminars
Arts and crafts exhibits and fairs first weekend
in July

❖ **Rural Rembrandts**
Geraldine Dobs
4278 Alpine Dr, RR 2 Box 663-7, Wautoma,
WI 54982
414/787-4568

Public art organization
Competitions
Art library

CHAPTER VIII
CRITICS

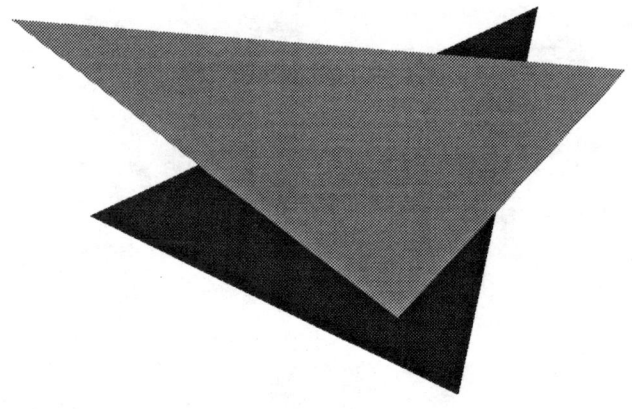

Meet the Press

At some point as you are starting your career, you should make direct contact (via phone) with your local art editors and reviewers. They will be an important source for familiarizing the public with your name. It is necessary to get coverage over and over again. People need to hear your name and see your work frequently to remember it.

Are you having a solo exhibition soon—in a gallery, exhibit space or perhaps an open studio? Make the most of it and get good press coverage! Use some ingenuity and think of a good "story-line" to lure an art editor to your doorstep for an interview, or at least to your show for a peek.

It is often necessary to send important reviewers and editors three mailings:

1. A press release—two months before the show
2. A personal invitation—one month before the show
3. A postcard reminder of the opening date—two weeks before the show.

Keep in mind that reviewers might not come to the actual opening. They might want to view your work in a quieter setting—before or after the opening. Some artists suggest that the reviewer contact them for a personal tour of the show.

Developing Your Press Kit

Editors are in constant need of a unique story. They often need a tidbit of information to fit a small space in their paper. They frequently copy verbatim from a press release for these small filler spaces, so make sure your press releases are well edited! Remember that you have competition, and you want your press kit to look professional (no typos or cross-outs).

Press Kit Contents

• Press release—just the facts, not too many embellishments. Make it easy for the editor to read. You can highlight in bold type the key information—artist's name, opening and closing dates and hours of exhibition, location (including town). Use your unique letterhead.

• Story line—supply them with a great "story-line" and you probably will lure them to your studio for an interview. What is a "story-line"? Something that is unusual and newsworthy about you, your life or your art—i.e. you began painting in your studio in the winter with no heat or electricity; you have two children and paint in the kitchen while they are running around; your paintings are produced on leaves; you mix your

colors by hand in the old-fashioned techniques of the masters, etc. Put on your thinking cap and discover what you do that is interesting! You can note at the end of your story-line that you're willing to be interviewed.

• Resumé - biographical documents, vitae, etc.

• B&W photograph (usually 5x7" or 8x10" so the newspaper can reproduce it) of yourself or a piece of work being shown. A picture is said to increase your chances of publicity quite a bit, but don't expect the photos returned. Horizontal photographs are preferred generally to vertical. Use a sticker (never write directly on the back or front of a photo) on the back of the photo to identify the subject, event name, contact person and who took the photo. Write in your caption (remembering it might be changed). The more unusual or curious the photo, the more likely it will be used, and the more likely people will stop to look at it.

• Folder—to complete the kit, use a simple folder to put all the papers in and keep them tidy. This folder adds a certain finality and intention to the press kit. If there is a catalog of the exhibit, include this in the folder.

Contacting the Press

The next step is to make sure the press kit reaches the correct people. Your mailing list should be compiled in a personal, methodical way. Make a note on your file card for each publication when you need to send your first press release. Knowing your editorial deadlines could be the most important matter involved. Monthly and weekly magazines have longer lead times, so you will need to send them earlier than the local newspaper. Don't forget the gallery guides, shoppers' guides and entertainment guides. You might want to send your press kit to several editors at a local newspaper; art, entertainment, style, weekend section, etc. Once you get your mailing list down, you will be able to use it over and over again for other events.

General Pointers

• Schedule your opening day a few days after you expect to have the show hung. You will be able to get the oddities ironed out by that time.

• If you should be approached by two well-known publications in your area (or broadcast stations) only give one (of each type of media) a story. You want an 'exclusive' as it will enhance your credibility. The next time you can go with the other editor, if you feel it would be better to change.

Critics

- *Follow-up calls are important and can make the difference in whether you get publicity or not. It's important to call editors when they are not rushing to meet a tight deadline. The best time to call is after a publication deadline or after a broadcast. Morning papers should be called mid-morning, afternoon papers mid-afternoon.*
- *If a mistake should occur in your article, inform the editor as soon as possible so that they can print a correction in the next publication.*
- *Whenever you do get an interview or coverage, be sure to write a thank you note to the person who was responsible. They will remember this! A personal phone call would be great, too.*
- *A show is not the only reason to contact media. Community service (donating a piece to a charity), changes in your business, awards and human interest can be other reasons. Try to develop your own reasons!*

Publications

See pages 74-76 for telephone numbers and addresses of publishers with asterisk following name.

Bulletproof News Releases
 Franklin-Sarrett Publishers
 3761 Vineyard Trl, Marietta, GA 30062
 800/444-2524
Practical advice for small businees. Lists 135 American newspaper editors. $18.95ppd.

Expose Yourself: How to Use Public Relations to Promote Yourself & Your Business by Melba Beals

Fine Art Publicity by Susan Abbott
 916/432-7630
$39.95.

Getting Publicity by Tana Fletcher sand Julia Rockler
 Self-Counsel Press*

Guerrilla P.R. by Michael Levine
 HarperCollins*

How to Get Results with Publicity
 700 Black Horse Pike #110, Blackwood, NJ 08012

Marketing Made Easier: Guide to Free Product Publicity
 Todd Publications
 914/358-6213
$25.00.

Marketing Without Money by Nicholas E Bade
 NTC Business Books*
Free and/or cheap offbeat ways for small businesses to increase sales.

Pocket Media Guide
 307 W 36th St, New York, NY 10018
Lists national media sources. Free if requested on business letterhead.

Power Marketing for Small Business by Jody Hornor
 PSI Research*
Have several books on business and marketing.

The Publicity Kit by Jeanette Smith

Six Steps to Free Publicity/66 Ways to Make You or Your Business Newsworthy
 Marcia Yudkin
 PO Box 1310, Boston, MA 02117
$6ppd/4 pages of information.

Publicity Firms

(See page 23)

Critics

Some critics are connected with newspapers and some are free-lancers, listed alphabetically by state and then city.

Barbara Periam
6536 Cheney Dr, Paradise Valley, AZ 85253

Phoenix Art Museum
Bruce Kurtz
1625 N Central Ave, Phoenix, AZ 85020

Scottsdale Progress
Jennifer Franklin
7320 E Earl Dr, Scottsdale, AZ 85251

Pine Bluff Commercial
June Freeman
9 Southern Pines Dr, Pine Bluff, AR 71603

Patrick Prince
160 W Jaxine Dr, Altadena, CA 91001

Anaheim Bulletin
Tim Sosbe
1771 S Lewis St, Anaheim, CA 92805

Daily Ledger
Clay Kallam
PO Box 2299, Antioch, CA 92814

Bakersfield Californian
Rick Heredia
1707 Eye St, Bakersfield, CA 93301

Ramsey Bell Breslin
1298 Monterey Ave, Berkeley, CA 94707

Charles Shere
1824 Curtis St, Berkeley, CA 94702

Jacquelyn Silverman
426 So Peck Dr, Beverly Hills, CA 90210

Bill Berkson
PO Box 389, Bolinas, CA 94924

Chico Enterprise-Record
Gary Kupp
400 E Park Ave, Chico, CA 95926

Costa Mesa Pilot
Lauri Mendenhall
330 W Bay St, Costa Mesa, CA 92627

David Antin
PO Box 1147, Del Mar, CA 92014

Daily Californian
Karen Barnett
1000 Pioneer Way, El Cajon, CA 92022

Fidel Danieli
PO Box 410, El Portal, CA 95318-0410

Escondido Times
Louise Omdash
207 E Pennsylvania, Escondido, CA 92025

Eureka Times Standard
Kathy Dillon
930 6th St, Eureka, CA 95501

Fairfield Daily Republic
Ted Hoffman
1250 Texas St, Fairfield, CA 94533

Fresno Bee
David Hale
1626 E St, Fresno, CA 93786

Glendale News-Press
David Perry
111 N Isabel, PO Box 991, Glendale, CA 91209

Daily Review
Barry Caine
116 W Winton Ave, Hayward, CA 94544

Long Beach Museum
Nancy Drew
2300 East Ocean Blvd, Long Beach, CA 90803

Long Beach Press-Telegram
Todd Cunningham
604 Pine Ave, Long Beach, CA 90844

Syd Cassyd
917 S Tremaine Ave, Los Angeles, CA 90019

Peter Clothier
2341 Ronda Vista Dr, Los Angeles, CA 90027

Peter Frank
PO Box 24A35, Los Angeles, CA 90024-1036

Critics

Colin Gardner
1015 N Edinburgh Ave #2, Los Angeles, CA
90046

James Hugunin
629 Quail Dr, Los Angeles, CA 90065

Christopher Knight
6851 Iris Cir, Los Angeles, CA 90068

Michael Laurence
1736 3/8 Griffith Park Blvd, Los Angeles, CA
90026

Art Issues
Gary Kornblau
8721 Santa Monica Blvd #535, Los Angeles,
CA 90069

California Press Bureau
Lee Soble
6399 Wilshire Blvd #200, Los Angeles, CA
90048

LA Herald Examiner
Christopher Knight
1111 S Broadway, Los Angeles, CA 90015

LA Weekly
Peter Frank
PO Box 24A36, Los Angeles, CA 90024-1036

Los Angeles Opinion
Juan Rodriguez
411 W 5th St, Los Angeles, CA 90013

Los Angeles Reader
David Ulin
5550 Wilshire Blvd #301, Los Angeles, CA
90036-3389

Los Angeles Times
William Wilson/Suzanne Muchnic
Michael Dooley/Oscar Garza/Henry Seldis
Mirror Square, Los Angeles, CA 90053

New Art Examiner
Richard Smith
600 Moulton Ave #304, Los Angeles, CA
90031

Martinez News Gazette
Harriet Burt
615 Estudillo St, Martinez, CA 94553

Yuba-Sutter Appeal-Democrat
Julie Watson
1530 Ellis Lake Dr, Marysville, CA 95901

Merced Sun-Star
Colleen Bondy
3033 N G St, Merced, CA 95340

Modesto Bee
Leo Stutzin
Box 3928, Modesto, CA 95352

Herald
Rick Dergon
Pacific at Jefferson, Monterey, CA 93940

Napa Register
Mary Wallis
Box 150, Napa, CA 94559-0150

Marin Co Independent Journal
Phyllis Bragdon
Alameda Del Prado 150, Novato, CA 94947

Melinda Levine
456 61st St, Oakland, CA 94609

Mark Levy
3555 Monterey Blvd, Oakland, CA 94619

Oakland Tribune
Harriet Swift
1203 Preservation Pky #103, Oakland, CA
94612

No City Blade Tribune
Ramona Hattendorf
1722 S Hill St, Oceanside, CA 92054

Ontario Daily Report
Jerry Rice
2041 E Fourth St, Ontario, CA 91764

Santa Maria Times
Karen White
3200 Skyway Dr, Orcutt, CA 93455

Oxnard Press Courier
Lisa McKinnon
300 W 9th St, Oxnard, CA 93939

Marjorie Perloff
1467 Amalfi Dr, Pacific Palisades, CA 90272

Critics

The Desert Sun
Bruce Tessier
611 S Palm Canyon Dr, Palm Springs, CA
92262

Antelope Valley Press
Steve Hendrickson
37414 N Sierra Hwy, Palmdale, CA 93550

Betty Brown
1231 N Wilson Ave, Pasadena, CA91104

Richard Hertz
PO Box 7197, Pasadena, CA 91109

Melinda Wortz
580 Prospect Blvd, Pasadena, CA 91103

Star News
Kathy Register
525 E Colorado Blvd, Pasadena, CA 91109

Umbrella
Judith Hoffberg
PO Box 40100, Pasadena, CA 91114

The Herald
Joan Boer
4770 Willow Rd, Pleasanton, CA 94566

Redding Record
Laura Christman
1101 Twin View Blvd, Redding, CA 96049

Morning Press Enterprise
Loretta Scott
3512 14th St, Riverside, CA 92501

Sacramento Bee
Scott Lebar
21st & Q Streets, Sacramento, CA 95813

Salinas Californian
Tom Leyde
123 W Alisa St, Salinas, CA 93901

San Bernardino Sun
Owen Sheeran
399 N D St, San Bernardino, CA 92401

Mary Stofflet
3560 1/2 Fifth Ave, San Diego, CA 92103

San Diego Tribune
PO Box 191, San Diego, CA 92112

San Diego Union
Lee Grant/Robert Pincus
PO Box 191, San Diego, CA 92112-4106

Alan Bamberger
2510 Bush St, San Francisco, CA 94115

Whitney Chadwick
1600 Holloway Ave, San Francisco, CA
94132

Hal Fischer
117 Pierce St, San Francisco, CA 94117-3306

Thomas Gladysz
1518 Church, San Francisco, CA 94131

San Francisco Bay Guardian
Harry Roche
520 Hampshire St, San Francisco, CA 94110

San Francisco Chronicle
901 Mission St, San Francisco, CA 94103

San Francisco Examiner
David Bonetti
110 5th St, San Francisco, CA 94103

Bernice Scharlach
8702 Lomas Azules Pl, San Jose, CA 95135

San Jose Mercury News
Dorothy Burkhart/Robin Doussard/Nora
Villagran
750 Ridder Park Dr, San Jose, CA 95190

San Luis Obispo Telegram
Tony Hazarian
PO Box 112, San Luis Obispo, CA 93406

San Mateo Times
Mary Helen McAllister
1080 S Amphlett Blvd, PO Box 5, San Mateo,
CA 94402

San Pedro News Pilot
362 W 7th St, San Pedro, CA 90731

Orange Co Register
Barbara O'Dair
625 N Grand Ave, Santa Ana, CA 92701

Critics

Santa Barbara News Press
Gary Robb
De La Guerra Plaza, Santa Barbara, CA
93101

Alfred Jan
153 Kiely Blvd, Santa Clara, CA 95051-7019

Santa Cruz Sentinel
Rick Chatenever
207 Church St, Santa Cruz, CA 95060

Merle Schipper
835 Grant Ave #3, Santa Monica, CA 90405

Stockton Record
Janet Krietemeyer
530 E Market St, Stockton, CA 95202

Daily Breeze
Jim Brooks
5215 Torrance Blvd, Torrance, CA 90509

Victor Buck
952 W 9th St, Upland, CA 91786

Vallejo Times Herald
Zilleh Bahar
800 Curtola Pkwy, Vallejo, CA 94590

Scott Greiger
1419 Washington Blvd, Venice, CA 90291

Ventura City Star
Rita Moran
5250 Ralson St, Ventura, CA 93003

Victor Valley Press
Rae Dawn Olbert
13891 Park Ave, Victorville, CA 92392

Contra Costa Times
Carol Fowler
2640 Shadelands Dr, Walnut Creek, CA
94598

San Gabriel Valley Tribune
Johnny Bender
1210 Azusa Canyon Rd, West Covina, CA
91790

Daily Democrat
Mary Goetz
702 Court, Woodland, CA 95695

SouthWest Art
Gary Michael
3009 E 10th Ave, Denver, CO 80206

Larry Rinder
103 Great Plain Rd, Danbury, CT 06810

Shirley Gonzales
1949 Durham Rd, Guilford, CT 06437

Mimsie Coleman
57 Swarthmore St, Hamden, CT 06517

Kenworth Moffett
98 Old Long Ridge Rd, Stamford, CT 06903

Lee Fleming
1924 Park Rd NW, Washington, DC 20010

Andrew Hudson
1862 Mintwood Place NW, Washington, DC
20009

Museum Modern Art/Latin America
Jose Gomez-Sicre
1756 Lanier Pl NW Washington, DC 20009

Ft Lauderdale News & Sun
Roger Hurlbert
101 N River Drive, Ft Lauderdale, FL 33301

News Press
Mary Faulkner
2442 Anderson Ave, Ft Myers, FL 33901

Sun Sentinel/West Plus
Paul Idelberg
7139 W Oakland Pk Blvd, Lauderhill, FL
33313

Miami Herald
Bea Moss
PO Box 014699, Miami, FL 33101-9834

Orlando Sentinel
Chuck Twardy
PO Box 2833, Orlando, FL 32802-2833

Marcia Corbino
1111 N Gulfstream Ave #6B, Sarasota, FL
34326

Sarasota Herald Tribune
Joan Altabe
801 S Tamiami Trail, Sarasota, FL 34237

Tallahassee Democrat
Betty Rubenstein
277 N Magnolia Dr, Tallahassee, FL 32301

Sun Sentinel
Chauncey Mabe
15107 97 Rd N, West Palm Beach, FL 33412

Atlanta Journal
Catherine Fox
72 Marietta St, Atlanta, GA 30303

Dekalb News
Marge Price
739 DeKalb Industrial, Way, Decatur, GA 30033

Honolulu Star-Bulletin
Lois Taylor
605 Kapiolani Blvd, Honolulu, HI 96813

Idaho State Journal
Joy Morrison
PO Box 431, Pocatello, ID 83204-0431

Judith Russi Kirschner
5686 S Blackstone Ave, Chicago, IL 60637

Chicago Tribune
Alan Artne
435 N Michigan #414, Chicago, IL 60611

Peninsula Times Tribune
Jane Ayres
435 N Michigan Ave, #1609, Chicago, IL 60611-4008

Janice Langdon
12632 Anderson Rd, Granger, IN 46530

Holly Day
1207 Golden Hill Dr, Indianapolis, IN 46208

Mark E Stegmaier
1609 Pineacre, Davenport, IA 52803

Morning Advocate
Anne Price
525 Lafayette, Baton Rouge, LA 70802

The Times
Jo Ann Harris
222 Lake St, Shreveport, LA 71101

Daniel Grant
19 Summer St, Amherst, MA 01002
413/549-4312

Boston Globe
Kenneth Wise
135 William Morrisey Blvd, Boston, MA 02125

Detroit News
Joy Colby
615 W Lafayette, Detroit, MI 48231

Gerhardt Magnus
724 Rosewood Ave E, Lansing, MI 48823

Kansas City Star
Donald Hoffman
18th & Grand Ave, Kansas City, MO 64108

World Herald
Kyle MacMillan
13th & Dodge, Omaha, NE 68102

Sidney Rothman
2105 Central Ave, Barnegat Light, NJ 08006

James Youtz
11 Birchwood Rd, Bedminster, NJ 07921

Newark Star Ledger
Eileen Watkins
One Star Ledger Pl, Newark, NJ 07101

Gary Bascom
206A Union Ave, Rutherford, NJ 07070

The East Hampton
Rose Sinka/Helen Rahray
153 Main St, E Hampton, NY 11937-2716

Arts Magazine
Judy Collischan
141 W 21 St, Huntington Station, NY 11746

Judith Aminoff
40 Harrison St, New York, NY 10013

Jan Anderson
241 Central Park W, New York, NY 10024

Jane Bell
80 Wooster St, New York, NY 10012

Critics

Phyllis Braff
333 E 55th St, New York, NY 10022

Karen Chambers
One Sheridan St, New York, NY 10014

Cyril Christo
157 W 78 St, New York, NY 10024

Edit Deak
149 Wooster St, New York, NY 10012

Clement Greenberg
275 Central Park W, New York, NY 10024

John Gruen
317 W 83rd St, New York, NY 10024

Lisa Liebmann
3 E 69th St, New York, NY 10021

Miranda McClintic
1060 5th Ave, Apt 3D, New York, NY 10128

Jane Rankin
14 Delancy St, New York, NY 10002

Nancy Rosen
180 West 58th St, New York, NY 10019

Robert Rosenblum
33 W 10th St, New York, NY 10011-8726

Irwing Sandler
100 Bleecker St #30A, New York, NY 10012

Meyer Schapiro
279 W 4th St, New York, NY 10014

Jeanne Siegel
60 Sutton Pl S, New York, NY 10022

Carol Squiers
218 Thompson St, New York, NY 10012

Charles Stuckey
9 E Broadway, New York, NY 10038

Phyllis Tuchman
340 East 80th St, New York, NY 10021

Karen Wilkin
28 W 38th St, New York, NY 10018

Ann Sargent Wooster
170 2nd Ave, New York, NY 10003

Art in America
Lucy Lippard/Roberta Smith/Peter Schieldahl
575 Broadway, New York, NY 10012

Art in America/Art News
Gemit Henry
265 W 90th St #7, New York, NY 10024

Artist Associates
Bill Erlacher
211 E 51 St, New York, NY 10022

Barbara Gordon Association
165 East 32nd St, New York, NY 10016

George Borchardt Inc
John Ashbery
136 E 57th St, New York, NY 10022

Gralla Publications
Joe Termini
1515 Broadway, New York, NY 10030

MOMA
Todd Alden
11 West 53rd St, New York, NY 10019

Queens College
William Wilson
458 W 25th St, New York, NY 10001-6502

Russian Art Center
Margarita Tupitsyn
145 Chambers St, New York, NY 10007

School of Visual Arts
Shelly Rice
209 E 23rd St, New York, NY 10010-3994

Time Magazine
Robert Hughes
127 Ave of the Americas, New York, NY 10020

Village Voice
Richard Goldstein
842 Broadway, New York, NY 10003

David Shapiro
3001 H Hudson Parkway, Linden House #3B,
Riverdale, NY 10463

Robert Morgan
1237 E Main St, Rochester, NY 14609

Just Rochester
One Long Memorial Dr, Rochester, NY 14623

Martin Ries
36 Livingston Road, Scarsdale, NY 10583

Jack Bankowsky
97 Fort Pl, Staten Island, NY 10301-2334

Allen Coleman
465 Van Duzer St, Staten Island, NY 10304

Akron Art Museum
Barbara Tannenbaum
70 E Market , Akron, OH 44308

Beacon Journal
Dorothy Shinn
44 E Exchange, Akron, OH 44308

Daniel Brown Inc
2330 Kemper Ln, Cincinnati, OH 45206-2611

Taft Museum
Ruth Meyer
316 Pike St, Cincinnati, OH 45202

David Rubin
8501 Carnegie Ave, Cleveland, OH 44106

Plain Dealer
Steven Litt
1801 Superior Ave, Cleveland, OH 44114

Louise Bruner
4506 Indian Ridge, Sylvania, OH 43560

Broken Arrow Scout
Joan Rose
110 W Kenosha St, Broken Arrow, OK 74012

Uptown News
Celina Burkhart
4200 E Skelly Dr #970, Tulsa, OK 74135-3240

The Oregonian
Randy Gregg
1320 SW Broadway, Portland, OR 97204

Willamette Week
Greg Morris
2 NW 2nd Ave, Portland, OR 97209

Philadelphia Inquirer
Victoria Donahoe
34 Narbrook Park, Narberth, PA 19072

Roz Elman
4601 Bayard St #701, Pittsburgh, PA 15213

Pittsburgh-Post Gazette
Donald Miller
PO Box 957, Pittsburgh, PA 15230-0957

Pittsburgh Press
Patricia Lowry
34 Blvd of the Allies, Pittsburgh, PA 15222

Barbara Boyle Valentine
2025 Sunnyside Ave, Pottstown, PA 19464

Centre Daily Times
Dave Carty
PO Box 89, State College, PA 16804

Kenneth Baker
145 Prospect St, Providence, RI 02906

Clara Hieronymus
2200 Hemingway Dr, Nashville, TN 37215

Ronald Mintz
4917 Ravenswood Dr #1214, San Antonio, TX 78227-4342

Linda McGreevey
525 Pennsylvania Ave, Norfolk, VA 23508

The Leader
Jan Bauer
226 Adams, Pt Townsend, WA 98368

Milwaukee Journal
333 W State St, Milwaukee, WI 53203

Index

P

Packers   14, 21, 22
Palette   19
Paper   9, 14, 17-19, 77-78
Pastel   94
Pens   17, 19
Portfolios   9, 11, 14, 23
Pre-press   78
Press kits   121
Printer   71, 79-85
Promotion   10, 17, 19, 23
Publications   12, 15, 30, 31, 38-40, 49-64, 66-67, 69, 73, 75, 78, 125, 126, 136
Publicity   23
Publishing   13, 71

R

Recycling   14, 17
Reference directories   63-64
Regional directories   61-62
Restorers   23, 24

S

Sales agreement letter 30
Sales tax   29
SBA 29
Sculpture   40, 41, 45, 68, 88, 89, 102, 106
Slide labels   18, 25
Smocks   20
Software   11, 18
Specialty magazines   57-60
Stretcher bars   17, 20
Studio space   15, 89

T

Tapes   26, 27
Taxes   15, 29-35, 40, 71
Telephone   27
Theft   24

V

Video   11, 26, 27
Voicemail   27

W

Watercolor   18, 20, 78, 95-100
Wildlife   56, 75

WATCH OUT
FOR YOUR
FRIENDS!

THEY MAY STEAL
THIS BOOK,
UNLESS YOU BUY
THEM A COPY!

MAILING LISTS

ArtNetwork compiles lists of artworld professionals to sell it's own products. We also rent these clean and thoroughly composed lists to you! For a complete price break down and order form send us a SASE indicating you want a copy of our mailing list order form. Mail to ArtNetwork, PO Box 1268, 18757 Wildlfower Dr, Penn Valley, CA 95946. Some examples (prices are subject to change) of our lists are as follows:

48,000 artists . . . . $90 per 1000
3200 reps, consultants, dealers $195
1000 art councils $65
2900 art publishers $185
250 art publications $45
2120 art school art departments $140
6500 galleries . . . . $65 per 1000
2600 frame and poster galleries $175
750 foreign galleries $55
2800 art organizations $182
870 museum store buyers $65
1400 record companies $90
430 book publishers $45
265 photo galleries $45
1100 greeting card publishers $70

A r t N e t w o r k

The source for all your art marketing needs.

ArtSource Quarterly
Send $6 for the current issue.
ArtWorld Hotline
Send $2 for the current issue.
Art Marketing Handbook for the Fine Artist
$24.95+ $4 shipping
Art Marketing Sourcebook, Second Edition
$21.95+ $4 shipping (August 1995 publication date)
Seminars
Held throughout the country.
Encyclopedia of Living Artists
The10th anniversary edition will be coming out in 1997.
To participate send a SASE for a prospectus.
Cover contest
Be a winner of our bi-annual cover contest for the
Encyclopedia of Living Artists.
Consultations
Constance Smith, owner of ArtNetwork, conducts
private phone or mail consultations.
$30 for 30 minutes/$50 per hour.

Forthcoming books in 1996:
Business Forms for Fine Artists
Business Plans for Fine Artists
Making It Legal

Free Brochure

For a free brochure on all the above materials, send a
6x9 or larger SASE with 55¢ postage to:
ArtNetwork
PO Box 1268, 18757 WIldflower Dr
Penn Valley, CA 95946
To order any of the above items with a credit card call
916/432-7630.

FREE
DIRECTORY
LISTINGS!

Help us with the next edition of *ArtNetwork Yellow Pages*. Did we miss your company in this edition? Is your favorite printer, art organization, paper company not listed? Don't let us forget the next time. Photocopy and mail us the information below so we can include your requests absolutely free!

CATEGORY_____   CATEGORY_____

_____   _____
NAME OF COMPANY   NAME OF COMPANY

_____   _____
DIRECTOR   DIRECTOR

_____   _____
ADDRESS   ADDRESS

_____   _____
CITY/STATE/ZIP   CITY/STATE/ZIP

_____   _____
TELEPHONE   TELEPHONE

Mail your information to:
ArtNetwork
PO Box 1268
18757 Wildflower Dr
Penn Valley, CA 95946

GET 25% OFF YOUR NEXT PURCHASE!

Recycle your out-of-date books

It's important to keep your information library current. We will be updating this book bi-annually, adding totally new information, as well as deleting out-of-date information. To help make it easier to find the most current information quickly, we are extending this special offer of 25% off the next edition.

All you need do is cut out and mail the title portion of the cover of this book for the next update (1997) and you'll get 25% off the price of the second edition. We are also making this offer on *Art Marketing Sourcebook for the Fine Artist, Second Edition* (published 8/95) and *Art Marketing Handbook for the Fine Artist, Second Edition* (tentative publication date of 1996). For current price and editions call us at 916/432-7630 or fax us at 916/432-7633.

ArtNetwork

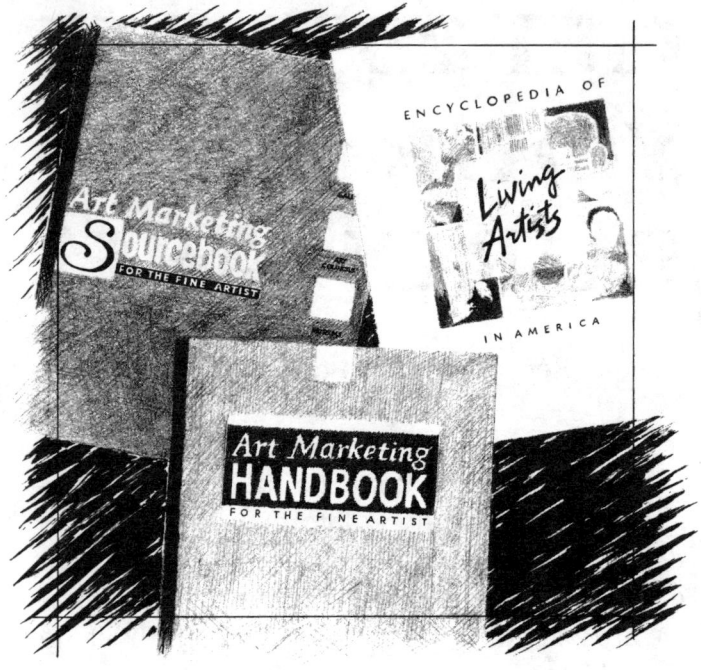

Linking the fine artist
to the artworld professional

▼

Mailing lists
Marketing books
Newsletters
Consultations
Seminars
Encyclopedia of
Living Artists

▲